THE MANHATTAN CHILI CO.™

SOUTHWEST AMERICAN
COOKBOOK

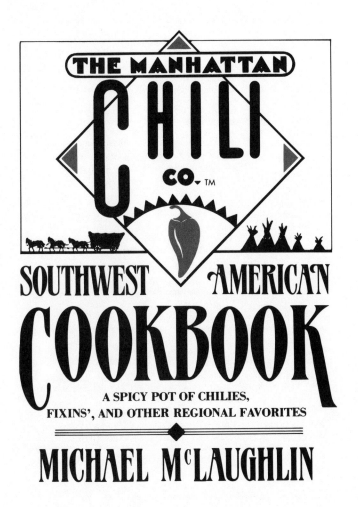

THE MANHATTAN CHILI CO. ™

SOUTHWEST AMERICAN COOKBOOK

A SPICY POT OF CHILIES, FIXINS', AND OTHER REGIONAL FAVORITES

MICHAEL M^cLAUGHLIN

Crown Publishers, Inc.
New York

FOR LUBA AND BRUCE, WITH SALSA

Grateful acknowledgment is given for the following recipes written by Michael McLaughlin:

"Fajitas of Grilled Pork with Chiles Chipotles" and "Chilled White Bean Soup with Lime and Cilantro" first appeared in the July 1985 issue and "Kahlúa Crème Brûlée" the August 1985 issue of *Bon Appétit*. Copyright ©1985 by Bon Appétit Publishing Corp. Used by permission of the publisher. "Seafood Chili San Carlos" first appeared in "Great Chef's Chili Dishes," by Richard Sax, in the February 1986 issue of *Bon Appétit*. Copyright ©1986 by Bon Appétit Publishing Corp. Used by permission of the publisher and author.

"Chocolate-Peanut Butter Mousse" first appeared in "Mostly Modern Mousses" in *Chocolatier Magazine*, Volume 1, Number 7. Copyright ©1986 by Chocolatier Magazine. Used by permission of the publisher.

"Three-Bean Vegetable Chili" first appeared in the *New York Daily News*. Copyright ©1985 by Michael McLaughlin. Used by permission of the publisher.

"The Real McCoy" and "Creating a Better Bowl of Red" (which appeared as "Tips on Making a Championship Bowl") appeared in the *New York Post*. Copyright ©1985 by Michael McLaughlin. Used by permission of the publisher. "The Real McCoy" also appears in *American Bistro*, by Irena Chalmers. Copyright ©1986 by Irena Chalmers Cookbooks, Inc. Used by permission of the author.

Published by Crown Publishers, Inc., 225 Park Avenue South, New York, New York 10003, and represented in Canada by the Canadian MANDA Group

CROWN is a trademark of Crown Publishers, Inc.

THE MANHATTAN CHILI COMPANY and logo, NUMERO UNO, THE REAL McCOY, TEXAS CHAIN GANG CHILI, ABILENE CHORAL SOCIETY AND MUSIC GUILD CHILI, SEAFOOD CHILI SAN CARLOS, HIGH PLAINS BUFFALO CHILI, and CALICO CORN MUFFINS are trademarks of The Manhattan Chili Company, Inc.

Manufactured in the United States of America

Design by Lauren Dong

Library of Congress Cataloging-in-Publication Data
McLaughlin, Michael.
    The Manhattan Chili Co. Southwest-American cookbook.
    "With 65 recipes."
    Includes bibliographies and index.
    1. Cookery, American—Southwestern style.
2. Manhattan Chili Co.   I. Manhattan Chili Co.
II. Title.   III. Title: Southwest-American cookbook.
TX715.M47435   1986   641.5'09747'1   86–6360
ISBN 0-517-56317-7

Original Manhattan Chili Co. logo designed by Darrell Beasley

10   9   8   7   6   5   4   3   2

CONTENTS

ABOUT THE BOOK:
An Introduction

This book is a record of two years in the restaurant business and half a lifetime interested in the foods of the American Southwest.

My first job, as an "adult," after leaving college, was as a waiter in an enormous Mexican restaurant, the first of its kind in an increasingly sophisticated college town in Colorado. From the minute it opened, it was a sensation. I know now that the food was acceptable at best, not particularly authentic, and of indifferent quality. Still, it was good enough to instill a love for even the lowliest of Tex-Mex menu items in me, a love I carry even today. Many visits to Arizona and Mexico followed over the years, and a considerable amount of tasting and testing went into the recipes for the restaurant I eventually opened.

This book is based upon that menu, but like any adaptation it has been "opened up." Items that for one complicated restaurant reason or another have never appeared or have disappeared or may one day appear on the menu are included here, to round out our view of some of the best of the traditional food we collectively call southwestern cooking.

Chili forms the heart of our menu, and it represents the major section of this book as well. Despite arguments to the contrary, chili, as we know it today, is an American original, both by virtue of the techniques with which it goes together and the way it combines typical southwestern ingredients. By now there is no such thing as authentic chili, although there is a comfortably wide set of accepted standards into which a spicy dish of mostly meat can fall and still be called chili. Within those standards I have enjoyed myself immensely. The chilies on our menu and in this book, while ranging far and wide, would never be mistaken for anything else.

Also included here are appetizers suitable for serving before chili, accompaniments to serve along with chili, and home-style desserts appropriate for enjoying after chili.

Another chapter is dedicated to southwestern fare other than chili. No attempt has been made to do more than barely scratch the surface here. Our restaurant is a casual one, and this book is meant to be casual, too, and, thus, such projects as making tamales or one's own corn or flour tortillas have been omitted on purpose. A good bookstore can supply any number of Southwest-American cookbooks which the eager perfectionist can consult to learn these fascinating techniques. That understood, the tastes and textures and smells of good southwestern food are explored and exploited with what I hope will be known as The Manhattan Chili Co. style.

Two friendly notes of warning. First, as with any discussion of regional cooking, great emphasis is made on certain ingredients. I have tried to be as generous in recommending substitutions as possible, and have included mail-order information for those ingredients for which there is no substitute. If you are interested in tasting this food as it is meant to taste, locating these ingredients is essential.

Second, while every attempt has been made to ensure that your home versions of our food will

BASICS

A SHORT BUT SPICY HISTORY OF AMERICA'S GREAT DISH

Like many of the world's great dishes of food—cassoulet, for example, or paella or pesto —chili inspires poetry, disagreement, and fanatical dedication. Like many of those dishes, it is essentially peasant food, having evolved to its present sophisticated form through a merely efficient use of ingredients at hand. Unlike virtually all of the other truly great dishes that come to mind, chili is an American original.

Chili's ancestral beginnings remain vague. Chiles—the colored fruits of the genus *Capsicum*—are natives of the Western Hemisphere, and were certainly combined by the Aztecs with meats and other ingredients in a zesty stew. Much later, some of the separate elements (chiles, cumin) crossed our southern border. It is known that the Indians of the southwestern United States pounded chiles and beef or venison into a kind of trail jerky. The insect-repellent qualities of the alkaloid capsaicin, present in chiles, helped preserve the meat on long journeys, and added savor to the reconstituted meal produced by simmering the jerky in water.

These same qualities undoubtedly inspired Texas-based trail-drive cooks, who needed to feed the hearty appetites of hard-working cowboys, to rekindle jaded palates numbed by weeks away from home, as well as to tenderize the tough but tasty beef of the original Texas longhorn.

As Texas shared the longest border with Mexico, so it claimed the credit for inventing chili, and the two have become irrevocably associated. Certainly the dish, as it is now prepared, bears little resemblance, either in technique or ingredients, to authentic Mexican cuisine.

Initially chili-making was somewhat hit or miss, the flavor and quality of whole chiles varying widely from place to place and year to year. The first ground chile was produced in Texas around 1890, greatly streamlining and homogenizing the chili-making process. This advance allowed the restaurant cook and later the home cook to easily and consistently duplicate the chili produced up to that time only by laborious hand-grinding or pureeing. Such efficiency made the transporting of chili's essential taste to the rest of the country inevitable. Texans can certainly claim to have "invented" chili, but there soon became not a state in the Union without chili lovers, chili parlors, and a more-or-less distinctive chili style of its own. Chili was simply too good for Texans alone.

By the 1920s chili was a readily familiar staple from coast to coast, the rakish participants in the Jazz Age flocking to sooth stomachs damaged by bootleg hooch with healing bowls of chili.

During the 1930s, chili, always an economical meal, provided inexpensive nourishment to a depressed country.

After World War II, chili welcomed hungry Americans home, with a taste of what was, by then, virtually the national dish.

The fifties may not have been chili's greatest era (it was a bland time), but chili certainly suffered no loss in popularity, and Joe Cooper's book, *With or Without Beans*, the first definitive chili book, was published.

By the 1960s, with the election of Lyndon

Johnson to the White House, chili was ready for a resurgence of interest that lasts today, nearly a hundred years after it first appeared in its current form.

Chili is available canned (240 million pounds of it in 1984), concentrated, and frozen. Restaurants, from the lowest beaneries to the hautest of establishments, offer it on their menus. Literally hundreds of chili cook-offs are held annually around the country. Books have been written, theses developed, ingredients debated, and reputations made and lost on the basis of a single spoonful of "Texas Red." Dozens of mixes and powders and kits (about seven million pounds a year) are marketed to enable one to re-create prize-winning recipes. Newspapers are devoted to the subject of chili's legend, lore, and continuing development. Societies have been formed to spread the word to Mexico, to Italy, to Japan. Can the same be said of paella or pesto or cassoulet?

CREATING A BETTER BOWL OF RED

CHILI STYLES

Any cook's attempts at creating a world-class chili, whether from scratch or by following a recipe, must begin with an understanding of basic chili styles. Similarly, the diner who digs a spoon into a Bowl of Red is in a better position to understand what he is eating if he recognizes the general direction from which the cook is coming. (Cinnamon, allspice, and ginger in your chili may outrage you if the traditional Cincinnati-style blend is unknown to you. Actually, it may *still* outrage you, but at least you'll have a better idea of who is to blame.)

The few chili styles below, simple though they are, reflect the widely differing philosophical approaches to America's great dish. Not surprisingly, many of the distinctions are regional.

Classic Texas

Typically tomato-less and bean-less (although plenty of Texans feel free to include both in their chili), this one is for purists. At its most primitive, it is nothing more than meat cooked with hot peppers. The passage of time and changing tastes have allowed such options as onions, garlic, cumin, and oregano to modify the rather carnivorous original into a rich and hearty stew. Although the meat—typically beef—can be coarsely ground, the most authentic results are achieved by using hand-diced meat.

Mainstream Americana

A rich, full-bodied brew, usually of ground beef, generous with tomatoes and beans. When the man on the street thinks of chili, this is the vision. Cumin, oregano, garlic, and onion are all but mandatory. Thickness or thinness of the final product varies with the cook, and spice levels range from Mid-Western Mild to New York Heat Wave, and all the stops between.

California Dreaming

Technicolor chili, light and lean, sometimes meatless or made with chicken and always featuring veggies (corn, avocado, black olives, 'shrooms, and fresh chiles, such as Anaheim or poblano) and lots of garnish—sour cream, cheese (Monterey Jack or chèvre), lettuce, bean sprouts, Maui onions, and so on and so on . . .

New Mexico/Arizona

Green chili, not red, heated up by fresh green chiles (no red powder here) and directly descended from Hopi and Navajo Indian stews. Pork or lamb (sometimes venison), in good-size chunks, are the preferred meats, while carrots, potatoes, and/or hominy round out a hearty (and usually sizzlingly hot) bowl of solid nourishment.

Cincinnati

This one reads better than it tastes. Although the notion of Middle Eastern spices sits well with chili's other essential ingredients, the thin, mild, slightly sweet stuff that predominates here is a local phenomenon that takes a lot of getting used to. On the other hand, as a justification for using sweet spices to power a bowl of *real* chili (see Numero Uno, page 42, or Lamb Chili on a Bed of Jalapeño Hominy, page 57) the concept is indispensable.

Mondo Chili

With a little luck, as many a chili cook-off runner-up has learned, you can throw almost anything into an otherwise well-constructed pot of chili and still get something edible. Occasionally, the results are an improvement, but too often such frisky experimentation is eccentricity for its own sake. The success of the resulting chili is usually directly proportionate to the number of Margaritas the tasters have enjoyed. I keep a file; interested readers are encouraged to submit oddities they have known. Consider: barbecue sauce, aquavit, rattlesnake meat, cigar ashes, dill, brown sugar, Italian sausage, fennel seeds, woodruff, lima beans, maple syrup, Parmesan cheese, bitters, curry powder, escargots, water chestnuts, dry sherry, corned beef, currant jelly . . .

CHILI TECHNIQUE

The basic technique of chili-making is so simple as to be primitive, and is clearly little changed from when those trail-drive cooks suspended a batch of chili in a cast-iron pot over an open fire.

A heavy pan—of cast iron if you wish—is ideal for the lengthy simmering needed to produce good chili. You won't need the lid; our chilies are always cooked uncovered. If the recipe calls for wine, vinegar, or other acidic ingredients, select a nonreactive pan, such as enameled cast iron, anodized aluminum, or tin-lined copper.

7

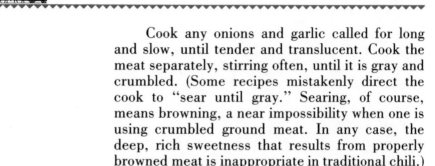

Cook any onions and garlic called for long and slow, until tender and translucent. Cook the meat separately, stirring often, until it is gray and crumbled. (Some recipes mistakenly direct the cook to "sear until gray." Searing, of course, means browning, a near impossibility when one is using crumbled ground meat. In any case, the deep, rich sweetness that results from properly browned meat is inappropriate in traditional chili.) The meat *should* be cooked until gray, unappetizing as that sounds, and stirred constantly until fully and evenly crumbled. Any ground meat not so cooked will transform itself into a bland meatball in the middle of your otherwise spicy chili—a *faux pas* if ever there was one.

You then combine the meat and onions (in the chili pot) with chili powder and dry spices and cook, stirring, over low heat for a few minutes. While this may or may not bring out more of the spices' flavors, it *seems* to me that it does, and I never omit this step. All that then remains is to add any liquids (including tomatoes) and simmer until "done."

Unless ordered to by one's coronary specialist, the grease that rises to the surface of the chili as it cooks should not be removed. Much of the flavor and heat are concentrated there, and removal will result in an indifferent, if not downright insipid, chili. Cornmeal stirred into the chili near the end of the cooking time will act as a thickener and as a "tightener" or "binder," absorbing the delicious but unattractive oil slick and dispersing it throughout the chili. Add the cornmeal by eye, using just enough to vanquish the grease, if you like a thinner chili, or even more, after the grease is absorbed, if you like a thicker chili. To some extent this is the cook's choice, but you will also be at the mercy of the fat content of the meat your butcher has sold you, since a greasier chili, before binding, will be a thicker chili afterward, and so on. One friend, not very well brought up, I admit, thinks chili *should* be greasy, and wouldn't dream of disguising the fact.

On the other hand, those who must degrease should omit the cornmeal and refrigerate the chili overnight (anyway, it *does* taste better the next day); the hardened fats will then lift off easily. Only then should cornmeal be added, as a thickener only. Some slight overcompensation when measuring the spices will do much toward avoiding blandness in a de-fatted chili, although a certain lack of "meatiness" is unavoidable.

Another solution to the problem of greasy chili is to begin with very lean meat (ground, not cubed, which will become dry) and pour off onion cooking oil and any fat. Add the liquids *and then* the dry spices, and use water instead of beef broth or stock. Tougher cuts of lean veal, such as shank, make good chili.

CHILI INGREDIENTS

Since the actual technique of chili-making is so simple, why is there so much bad chili in the world? The answer lies in how easy it has become to throw together a mediocre batch. One quick, lazy trip through the modern supermarket will provide the supplies for a numbingly ordinary pot of chili—hamburger meat, commercial chili powder, dehydrated onions, prechopped garlic, stewed tomatoes, mushy beans, even synthetic sour cream, as ersatz garnish. One hardly has to think to assemble this dreary concoction, and one would be well advised not to think at all while ingesting it. If the results of all that labor taste canned anyway, why not just buy canned chili?

On the other hand, attention paid when as-

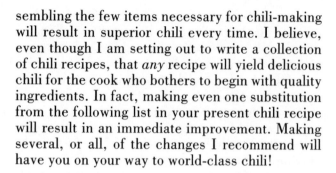

sembling the few items necessary for chili-making will result in superior chili every time. I believe, even though I am setting out to write a collection of chili recipes, that *any* recipe will yield delicious chili for the cook who bothers to begin with quality ingredients. In fact, making even one substitution from the following list in your present chili recipe will result in an immediate improvement. Making several, or all, of the changes I recommend will have you on your way to world-class chili!

Meat

Beef is classic, although good chili can be made with any full-flavored meat. Versions using lamb, pork, venison, and buffalo are included in the recipe section. Whatever you use, avoid deluxe cuts of meat; they will turn to mush during that essential long simmer. Shank, chuck, shoulder, etc., are preferable to, say, fillet. A small proportion of fat is desirable, too, for the best flavor. The meat should be diced by hand into ½-inch cubes or ground by your butcher through the coarsest grinder disk he has. Ours uses a disk with ⅜-inch holes, but he ordered it especially for us. Typically, a butcher who makes his own Italian sausage will have a slightly finer grinding disk that will still produce meat superior to ordinary hamburger, which, again, will result in mushy chili.

Order in advance to avoid disappointment. Some city or state health department rules forbid grinding meat this coarse (if the butcher is careless, bone chips can pass through these large grinder holes), and, if your meat includes pork, the butcher will have to clean the machine after grinding your order, to avoid mixing pork with future batches of ground beef, a chore some refuse to perform for only a few pounds of meat. If civilization throws too many of these stumbling blocks in your way you might consider buying your own grinder, shopping carefully for a brand that offers a coarse blade, which you will still probably have to order. Cooks with a food processor equipped with a "pulse-type" switch can approximate these results on their own at home, chopping the meat in small batches with "on-and-off" motions and staying alert to avoid overprocessing. What a pleasure it is to walk into a supermarket in the Southwest and see coarse, chili-grind meat displayed ready to use between the pork chops and the pot roast!

Chili Powder

Read the label. Most commercial chili powders are blends—like curry powder—that spice companies think you want in your chili. We pursue purity here, and any serious chili cook will do the same. Use a mild, fresh, and flavorful, but otherwise unseasoned, chili powder, add cumin, oregano, garlic, and salt in the proportions *you* prefer, and let cayenne, jalapeños, or another independent source supply the heat. You can also create a chili blend by combining New Mexico, California, ancho, and/or jalapeño powders to customize your chili even further. Mail-order sources for such powders are listed at the end of the book. Cumin et al. are still up to you. As you will see from the following recipes, my formula changes with each—a cranky independence that has frustrated more than one spice wholesaler who would like to sell me my own "chili blend," but who balks at the notion of making up a different one for every chili on the menu.

It is unlikely that such a pure chili powder

11

will appear in your supermarket. One good national brand (Jane Butel's Pecos River) is commonly found in department store food sections. Or you will have to locate a spice store or a mail-order source (page 115). Remember that even unseasoned powders can be blends of more than one kind of chile. You may have to try several before you find one you like, and you should also be aware that changing brands will usually change the chili. Serious cooks become a bit possessive of their favorite—championship chilies usually specify a name brand for best results—and I've used the same powder for nearly 10 years, both at home and in the restaurant. Mail ordering a batch from time to time seems a small price to pay for the resulting peace of mind.

Refrigerate your powder in an airtight container and try to use it up within six months or so. Some sources call for paprika if chili powder is unavailable. If you are certain you are getting genuine Hungarian paprika instead of the less-flavorful Spanish variety found in the typical supermarket, this will do in an emergency. I find a certain lack of real chili depth in paprika, and usually end up doctoring the chili extensively before I'm ready to serve it.

Cumin

This spice is as essential as chili powder. The generous use of cumin is a hallmark of Tex-Mex cooking, clearly separating it from the more subtle touch south of the border.

For all recipes in this book, cumin should be toasted, a simple enough process that will dramatically improve your chili, as well as any other dish calling for cumin. Buy whole cumin seeds. (You can mail order these from sources in the back of the book, but most supermarkets stock this product.) Prepare a quantity—it's easier to toast half a cup than a few tablespoons. Pour the seeds into a small heavy skillet and set over low heat. Stir often; in 7 to 10 minutes the cumin will be a rich, dark brown and smell wonderful. Do not allow the seeds to burn, and remove them from the skillet immediately. Store the seeds in a jar with a tight-fitting lid and grind them for each use. (I keep a small electric spice mill just for cumin.) Sieve the cumin if there are coarse pieces remaining un-ground *and then measure it* for the recipe. Its richer, mellower taste makes for superior chili.

Onions and Garlic

Some purists omit both. While chili without tomatoes can be delicious, chili with no tomatoes, onions, *or* garlic is a starkly carnivorous affair that will not appeal to many. Use big yellow globe on-ions for easier peeling. The same goes for garlic: The bigger the clove, the better. Instant, dehy-drated, or prechopped versions of either are for-bidden.

Tomatoes

Some chilies have them and some don't. I would rather let the Texans argue about whether or not tomatoes belong and save my energy for a second helping. We use good-quality Italian canned tomatoes, usually well drained and always in moderation. Crush them thoroughly—pieces of tomato floating in the finished product are inap-propriate, whether you're from Texas or not. One good compromise in the tomato controversy is to substitute 1 or 2 cups of tomato juice for the liquid called for in a recipe. Tomato paste, for my money, is too sweet.

Beans

Again, let the Texans do the talking. Sometimes beans are fine and other times they don't belong. Certainly a classic chili such as The Real McCoy should be beanless. On the other hand, the rich and spicy Numero Uno needs to be counterbalanced by the earthy neutrality of beans. Good-quality (firm, colorful) canned dark red kidney beans, well drained and added just at the end of the cooking time, are a more than acceptable convenience. Purists can soak the dried beans, cook them separately, and add them, like the canned, near the end of the cooking time.

Oregano

Not a requirement for good chili, though I personally find it essential. (I have friends, however, who deride any chili with oregano in it as spaghetti sauce.) Mexican oregano—wild marjoram—has a flavor unlike anemic supermarket brands. If you can locate it (again, in spice stores or specialty food shops, or by mail), use it; it makes a world of difference. (Food authority Elizabeth Schneider has suggested mixing ordinary oregano and marjoram, half and half, as a substitute—an excellent compromise.)

Cayenne Pepper

Once you have accepted the notion that chili powder is for flavor, you will need a separate heat source over which you can exercise some control. Cayenne pepper is readily available and remains my first choice. The heat level varies a lot between types and brands, and the admonition "to taste" really applies here. The quantities given in the following recipes are based on fresh, but rather ordinary, supermarket cayenne. If you have a dusty jar that has been at the back of your spice rack for years, obviously you will need to buy a fresh one. And, if you use the intensely hot African cayenne from Aphrodesia (90,000 Scoville units—a scientific measurement of "heat") we get for the restaurant, you will need a lot less. Taste often and proceed with caution: The expression "no pain, no gain" was *not* intended to refer to chili.

Chili Paste

There is currently a lot of snob appeal attached to using a puree of chiles in place of the dried powder. Like making one's own pasta or bread or preserves when there are plenty of better commercial versions around, making chili paste is the sort of thing one does to stay in touch with the cooking basics.

At the restaurant we use the Santa Cruz brand of commercially produced chili paste. It is a bright red, very mild paste, not unlike their chili powder.

For the curious I have included below the formula I use when I want to go to the trouble. This is not particularly authentic, as it combines several chiles not strictly associated with Tex-Mex cooking. I enjoy choosing and combining, however, because I think it puts me in charge of what goes into my chili, which is, after all, what this is all about.

Working with the whole chiles lends an air of the exotic that opening a jar of chili powder just can't match. The students who take my classes are always fascinated when I demonstrate this paste, and the resulting pot of chili always draws the most interest, whether for its taste or the work involved, I couldn't say.

15

Homemade Chili Paste
Makes about 2 cups chili paste

12 large New Mexico or California red chile pods
    (about 3 ounces)
3 cups water
2 to 3 large ancho chiles (about 2 ounces)
2 pasilla chiles (about 1 ounce)
6 guajillo chiles (about 1 ounce)
2 to 4 tablespoons adobo from canned chipotles

    1. Remove the stems from the chiles. Tear the chiles into ½-inch pieces and combine in a heatproof bowl. Bring water to a boil. Pour the water over the chiles, stir well, and cover. Let stand for 2 hours, stirring occasionally.
    2. Drain the chiles, reserving the liquid. Puree the solids in a food processor until smooth.
    3. Press the puree through a fine sieve to remove any unprocessed seeds or tough bits of skin. Stir in the reserved soaking liquid and the adobo from the chipotles. Cover tightly and refrigerate or freeze until ready to use.

    Two practical notes: Wear rubber gloves when handling any chiles, until you know you can do so without discomfort. Many people aren't bothered at all, while others will puff and swell and go through fairly severe reactions. In any case, keep the chiles well away from your eyes and face and other sensitive membranes and wash your hands well with lots of hot soapy water when you're through. Capsaicin, the alkaloid that produces the stinging sensation of heat in chiles, is oily and will cling to your skin for hours.
    Second, if you've gone to the trouble to mail order the dried chiles for the paste, make it up

fairly promptly and freeze it in suitable batches. Dried chiles are prone to get buggy very fast, and the best way of preventing the ruin of your supply is to get it into the freezer pronto. It will keep well there for at least six months.

The paste can be substituted in any recipe calling for powdered chile, using about 1 cup of paste for each ⅓ cup of powder. (The reverse substitution, however, won't work. If a recipe calls for chili paste, you must use paste, although it can be your own homemade paste or a purchased brand.) Inevitably there is variation when using whole dried chiles, and some flavor adjusting will be required after the paste is incorporated into the dish. (Also, the homemade paste given here is much hotter than commercial brands, and you should expect to reduce the cayenne or other "heat" elements in a recipe when you use it.) Such variation is part of the fun of this admittedly old-fashioned process.

Fresh Chiles

Although not, strictly speaking, part of chili tradition, fresh chiles are by now a common ingredient in many a chili pot. Their heat seems to affect the mouth and taste buds differently than, say, cayenne pepper, and they bring their own fresh, green flavor to the dish as well. Most commonly used (and most easily located) are the fat, green jalapeños, and we call for them in several chilies. The smaller, somewhat hotter serranos are also a good chili addition. The large poblano chile, used in the Green Chili given in this book, ranges from a rather bell pepper-like sweetness to very picante and has a flavor that makes it one of the most satisfying chiles to cook with and to eat. See page 51 for directions on roasting (or "parching") poblanos before use.

Canned Chiles

Since I nearly always lug a shopping bag of fresh jalapeños and poblanos with me when teaching classes around the country, I should point out that they are, except in communities with large Latin American populations, not easy to find, and it's perhaps better not to get too attached to using them. There are alternatives.

Canned jalapeños (usually packed in some sort of brine and labeled *en escabeche*, which means pickled) and "fire-roasted mild green chiles," usually of an unspecified type, are more widely available and will do in any recipe that calls for lengthy cooking. For uncooked dishes, such as guacamole or salsa, canned chiles, while only a poor compromise, are still better than using cayenne, which is too harsh when uncooked, or bottled hot sauces, with their intrusive fermented vinegary tang.

One chile—the chipotle—to which I grow increasingly addicted, is sometimes found dried, but is really at its most useful canned. These are red ripe jalapeños that have been smoked and then packed in a tomato-and-vinegar sauce or adobo. Wrinkled and a dusky brick red, the chiles are incredibly hot and the smoky afterbite is wonderful. We use them in our Nachos, for a unique twist on a standard Tex-Mex item, and they add their barbecue pungency to the tomato sauce for our Fajitas recipe. Either the chiles themselves, or just the adobo, will put real kick in your homemade chili paste.

Options

Other secret ingredients can lead you to a fabulous batch of chili without crossing the border into Mondo land. Unsweetened cocoa or cooking chocolate adds color, flavor, and incomparable texture, especially in pork chili. A touch of cinna-mon will sweeten acidic canned tomatoes, adding a hint of mystery that the ubiquitous "pinch of sugar" can't provide. Beef or meat stock in place of water adds fuller flavor, making for a larger-than-life chili, as does beer—preferably a rich, dark beer. Dry red wine, used judiciously, will also have your guests smacking their lips and trying to guess your secret. A cup of black coffee, in true chuck-wagon fashion, will also get results; and tequila, in small doses, does "something" for the chili—perhaps the same thing it does for the cook. As with any experimental cooking, stir in a little, simmer for 5 to 10 minutes, and taste. Keep working, keep tasting (the best part), and write down the resulting changes. Nothing is more frus-trating than stumbling upon the perfect, univer-sally excellent bowl of The Ultimate Chili, snaffling up the entire batch, and then not remem-bering what made that elusive difference!

STORAGE

Assuming self-control, a finished batch of chili will keep quite a while. At least 24 hours refrigerated aging is recommended (we do this at the restaurant, despite the congestion it causes in our tiny walk-in refrigerator), and 48 is even bet-ter. However tasty a chili may be at the end of its simmer, it will be that much mellower and more "complete" with a little refrigerated rest.

On the long side of things, ten days of well-refrigerated storage is not out of the question (talk about self-control), and short-term freezing (up to a month) is no problem. Beyond that there is a diminution of flavor and a mushiness of texture that, while not fatal to the chili, somewhat dimin-ishes its charm.

OVER, UNDER, INTO, AND AROUND

A pot of chili at hand is only just the beginning for many people. Given all the ways chili can be spooned over, under, into, and around other foods, it seems downright old fashioned to merely eat it out of a bowl with a spoon. Here are some classics.

CHILI MAC

The truckstop special. Spoon heated chili over hot, cooked pasta (preferably elbow macaroni) in individual gratin dishes. Top generously with grated cheese and bake until melted and bubbly. Sprinkle with chopped onion before serving.

This arrangement gets complicated when served Cincinnati style. In that city's many parlors, one can choose the Two Way (beanless chili over pasta), Three Way (chili over pasta with cheese), Four Way (the Three Way, plus onions), and the ultimate Five Way—the Four Way, begun with a layer of beans.

In Texas, the chili/pasta combo is known as Spaghetti Red, and, despite some aversion (like that for beans), the combination is a good one. I have heard tell of, but have never seen, chili lasagne, about which the less said, probably, the better.

CHILI RICE

If anything, this is a more felicitous combination than chili and pasta. Whether merely spooned into the bowl alongside the chili, or used as the basis for constructions similar to the Two Way, and so on, listed above, fluffy white rice remains a classic—and my personal favorite—chili accompaniment.

WET SHOES

Chili over French fries is another pairing made in chili-parlor heaven. Although not classically offered with other adornments, a sprinkling of grated cheese and diced onion is not out of place here. Speaking of potatoes, try spooning chili over a hot, split baked potato and topping it with a dollop of cool sour cream.

CHILI PIE

Originally (according to one of our regular customers, the Lone Star News Hen), this was nothing more than a small bag of Fritos torn open, topped with chili, cheese, and onions, offered with a plastic spoon, and eaten right from the bag. Don't forget Frito-Lay is headquartered in Dallas. Nowadays, Chili Pie usually comes on a plate, but the basis is still corn chips of some kind, topped with chili. The cheese is melted and chopped onions are applied; then shredded lettuce, diced ripe tomatoes, sour cream, and guacamole gussy the thing up pretty good—prime junk food.

CHILI CASSEROLE

A Home-Ec cousin of Chili Pie. Spoon hot chili into a casserole dish. Top it with dollops of corn bread batter (or biscuit or dumpling dough) and bake until golden brown and bubbling.

CHILI BURGERS, CHILI DOGS, CHILI SIZE

These combinations illustrate a culinary rule of mine, McLaughlin's Law: The better something tastes, the harder it is to pick up. Chili dogs may have made Nathan's what it is today, but top-quality franks, burgers, and buns are needed to hold their own with homemade chili. Don't skimp. Onions, cheese, and so on are typical toppings. Pickle relish (or chopped sweet pickle) has a following as well.

Chili size is rather a different matter. A chili burger may be a sandwich, but chili size is something more elemental—a grilled or broiled patty of ground beef, topped with chili. Garnish or not. Meat-eaters only need apply.

SLIGHTLY MEXICAN

Chili makes an excellent taco filling. Spoon it into crisp shells (preferably ones you have fried yourself) and top with shredded lettuce, grated cheese, and Salsa Fresca (page 30). Or turn chili into burritos: Roll the chili up in warmed flour tortillas, including the lettuce, etc., inside, along with the chili. Munch, applying salsa as you go.

CHILI PIZZA

Why not combine two splendidly casual snack foods and let them complement each other? Chili, then cheese, makes a great pizza topping. For everything you need to know about pizza, consult Evelyne Sloman's *The Pizza Book* (Times Books). Her recipe for Lone Star Chili Pizza is on page 249.

CHILI EGGS

There are endless possibilities here. Top your bowl of chili with a fried or poached egg or two. Fold chili into an omelet. (At the Camelia Grill in New Orleans, the eggs for omelets are blended to a froth in malt machines, poured onto a griddle forming a rectangle the size of a bath mat, cooked to an ethereal lightness, and filled with chili and cheese before being folded up, business letter style, and served forth with French fries—highly recommended.) Add cheese and/or onions. Spoon chili over poached eggs (on English muffins?), or just enjoy a bowl alongside your eggs and hash browns—there's hardly a better way to start the day.

CHILI SALAD

There are various versions of this one, all incorporating lettuce in some way. We pile shredded romaine onto a crisp, flat tostada, and top it with a generous ladle of chili; then we add cheese, sour cream, and diced ripe tomatoes and scallions —a flat taco, in effect, and delicious.

BREAD, ETC.

McLaughlin's Law applies to many combinations of bread and chili, some meant to be picked up, however awkwardly, others knife-and-fork food. Try chili poured over thick slices of sourdough toast; stuffed into pita bread (plus lettuce, cheese, and salsa); spooned into hot dog buns, for the legendary Chili Bun; ladled over pancakes, waffles, crêpes (I only report this stuff, folks); lavished on a split and toasted bagel, and so on. The improvisational spirit of American cuisine is at its finest with chili on hand.

PUTTING IT ALL TOGETHER

Chili is the most democratic of dishes, and you can take it anywhere. Once you have a savory pot ready to eat, you have the makings for everything from a quick meal after a hard day to a black tie and champagne reception. The only limits here are supplied by your imagination. Just remember, everyone likes chili.

FIXIN'S

The same cantakerous sense of individuality that inspires the chili cook extends to the chili eater when the bowl finally hits the table. For the diner the fun is just beginning. The fixin's—garnishes or add-ons—can make or break (or at least significantly modify) the basic Bowl of Red. Our customers can't seem to eat chili without stirring in sour cream, onions (red, yellow, green), grated cheese (Cheddar, Monterey Jack, or both), diced tomatoes, pickled jalapeños, minced cilantro, diced avocado, and/or big chowder crackers. The properly prepared chili host will offer an array of at least three fixin's—and let guests do as they please.

WHAT TO DRINK

Again the matter is highly personal. I grew up wanting nothing but milk with chili, and it still seems *right* somehow, though I haven't drunk a glass of milk in years. Beer would be the national beverage of choice with chili, I think, and people who never drink beer on any other occasion will automatically order one with chili. The kind of beer is also up to the diner. Texas or Mexican beers are in the right spirit, but hardly necessary. If you're hosting a chili bash, ice a tub of several kinds. Include at least one dark beer and one crisp, light pilsner.

Champagne has a long chili tradition, too. It may be the combination of something earthy and basic with something classy and expensive, but the pairing is not uncommon. For best results, the champagne should not be an elegant and utterly dry wine, but something with a little fruity sparkle.

Of course, if you are used, as we are, to thinking of chili as serious food, then you may think of serious food wine as the best accompaniment. French wines seem, somehow, wrong with chili, but spicy, powerful California reds (Zinfandel, Petite Sirah, Merlot) or crisp, fruity spicy whites, such as Gewurtztraminer, are fine chili wines, especially if you have kept your chili's heat levels within socially acceptable limits. Don't waste good wine on a childishly palate-scorching chili. A soft drink of some kind is the more appropriate beverage.

And then there are Margaritas. Our customers love them and, in truth, the classic Margarita is a delicious thing. (Try this formula: Combine equal parts of good gold tequila, Cointreau, and fresh squeezed lime juice and shake with ice. Strain into a glass rimmed with coarse salt.) Even so, I can't help thinking that drinking cocktails with food is uncivilized. As a prelude to sitting down to a bowl or two of top-notch chili, though, a Margarita is hard to beat.

THE RECIPES

N THE BEGINNING

The ideal opener to a bowl of chili (or something equally hearty) should be imaginative, light, and piquant. This eclectic collection represents our attempts to keep the restaurant's menu lively and interesting, rather than any serious attempt at authentic southwestern cookery.

Ceviche
Serves 8

Most versions of this dish of raw, marinated seafood are unpleasantly hot and sour, masking the sweet delicacy of the fish. Avoid that error by discarding the lime juice that "cooks" the Ceviche and replacing it with a light Jalapeño Vinegar and olive oil dressing.

1½ pounds whitefish fillets
¼ pound bay scallops
¼ pound large shrimp, peeled and deveined
1 cup fresh lime juice (about 6 limes)
2 to 3 tablespoons Jalapeño Vinegar (page 83)
2 tablespoons good-quality olive oil
3 ripe but firm tomatoes
¾ cup finely chopped clean fresh cilantro leaves
½ cup finely diced red onion
Salt
2 heads romaine lettuce

1. Trim the fish fillets, discarding any tough or bony bits. Cut the fish into ½-inch pieces.

2. In a strainer under cold running water rinse the scallops and drain them well. Cut the shrimp in half crosswise. In a medium, deep bowl, combine the seafood and lime juice. Cover and refrigerate overnight, stirring once or twice when you think of it.

3. Drain the seafood thoroughly and discard the lime juice. Transfer the marinated seafood to a bowl, stir in the Jalapeño Vinegar and olive oil (gently, now that the fish is "cooked"), cover, and return the Ceviche to the refrigerator. The dish can be prepared to this point 4 hours before serving.

4. Just before serving, halve the tomatoes, squeeze out the liquid and seeds, and cut into ¼-inch dice. Gently stir the tomatoes, cilantro, and onion into the Ceviche. Taste and correct the seasoning, adding salt only if necessary, and, perhaps, a splash more vinegar.

5. To serve, separate the romaine into leaves. Wash, if necessary, and pat dry. Reserve the coarse, dark outer leaves for another use. Line each plate with two or three of the yellow inner leaves and mound the Ceviche on the leaves. Spoon any accumulated juices from the bowl over the Ceviche and serve at once. Offer guests a pepper mill at the table.

▼▼▼ NOTE: *This recipe will serve four as a main course: Spoon the Ceviche over a generous bed of mixed salad greens (such as romaine, watercress, or arugula) and drizzle with the accumulated juices as a dressing. Garnish with thin unpeeled wedges of ripe Haas avocado and thin rings of sweet red onion.*

Salsa Fresca
Makes about 3 cups

This is a very personal interpretation of the classic Mexican table sauce. While the flavor is authentic, the gazpacho-like texture is how it seems to me a salsa *should* be. Certainly it is more trouble this way (all that dicing) and we met a certain resistance at first for charging for an item that was free (but awful) at other Tex-Mex establishments. Now our regulars recognize it for what it is—a special appetizer worth enjoying for its own sake. Don't limit its use—we apply it liberally as a condiment with eggs, soups, salads, and chilies.

2 pounds (about 10) ripe Italian plum tomatoes,
    seeded, juiced, and cut into ¼-inch dice
    (you should have about 3 cups)
3 large fresh jalapeños, stemmed
⅓ cup finely chopped onion
½ cup tomato juice
Juice of 1 lime (about 3 tablespoons)
½ teaspoon salt
1 cup clean fresh cilantro leaves

    1. In a food processor fitted with a metal blade, combine *half* the tomatoes, the jalapeños, *half* the onion, the tomato juice, lime juice, and salt. Process until smooth and transfer the puree to a bowl.
    2. Stir in remaining tomato and onion. Finely chop the cilantro leaves, stir them into the salsa. Let stand at room temperature for 30 minutes before using.

▼▼▼NOTE: *For our purposes at the restaurant, Italian plum tomatoes are the most reliable and available. The point, however, is to use whatever tomatoes are available that are red, ripe, and full of flavor. If, at the height of summer, you are using tomatoes from your own garden, you will have a superlative salsa, and a wonderful condiment for almost anything that is charcoal grilled. Don't puree the cilantro leaves (the salsa will end up an ugly brown color) and don't make it more than 3 or 4 hours before you plan to use it: its sassy freshness is its principal virtue.*

Baked Goat Cheese with Salsa Fresca
Serves 6

If the familiarity of warm goat cheese dishes has bred a little contempt in you, try this approach for a change of attitude. The chunky, rustic raw salsa and the equally tangy and rustic goat cheese are perfect partners, aiding and abetting each other in producing a tasty first course. (This is not as cross-cultural a hodgepodge as you may think— there are Mexican cheeses with a similar salty tang.) We like the mild and creamy New York State goat cheese produced by Little Rainbow Chèvre, but any similar cheese will do as well. Offer unseasoned corn chips for scooping, or spread the warm cheese-and-salsa mixture on crusty bread.

12 ounces unaged, rindless, relatively mild goat
    cheese, such as Montrachet
2 cups Salsa Fresca (page 30)
Sprigs of fresh cilantro, as garnish

1. Preheat the broiler. Position the broiler rack about 6 inches from the heat source.

2. Cut the goat cheese into twelve equal disks. Set two disks in each of six individual broiler-proof gratin dishes. Broil the goat cheese, moving the dishes around to promote even cooking, until the edges of the disks are browned and the cheese is hot and sizzling, 3 to 4 minutes.

3. Transfer the gratin dishes to liner plates and let stand for 1 minute. (If the dishes are too hot the Salsa Fresca boils and splatters them unattractively.) Spoon the salsa evenly over and around the goat cheese, garnish each portion with a sprig of cilantro, and serve at once.

 Hot Wings
Serves 6 to 8

Hot, crisp, and spicy chicken wings, dipped into a cool, zesty sauce, seem to be a universal human craving not limited to Buffalo, New York. These were a recent addition to the menu, and from that first evening, we've had trouble keeping up with the demand. We serve them with the Green Dip that follows, but they're equally good with Salsa Fresca (page 30) or Salsa Mayonnaise (page 71).

Vegetable oil
⅓ cup yellow cornmeal
⅓ cup unbleached all-purpose flour
1 tablespoon ground cumin, from toasted seeds
1½ teaspoons salt
1½ teaspoons freshly ground black pepper
¾ teaspoon cayenne pepper
15 chicken wings (about 2½ pounds total weight)
Green Dip (recipe follows)

1. Preheat the oven to 375°F. Lightly brush a 12 × 17-inch jelly roll pan with vegetable oil.

2. In a medium bowl, combine the cornmeal, flour, cumin, salt, and black and cayenne peppers.

3. With a sharp knife, separate the wings into segments. Reserve the tip segments for another use.

4. A few at a time, turn the wing segments in the cornmeal mixture. Shake off the excess coating and arrange the wing segments, without crowding them, in the oiled pan.

5. Set the pan on an oven rack in the upper third of the oven. Bake the wings, turning once at the halfway point, for about 1 hour, or until they are crisp and evenly brown. Drain the wings briefly on paper towels and serve hot.

Green Dip
Makes about 3 cups

This is also delicious as a dip for cool poached shrimp and a nice change from salsa with corn chips.

3 cups clean fresh cilantro leaves
1 cup sliced scallions (including the green tops)
4 fresh jalapeños, stemmed and halved
1 tablespoon salt
2½ cups sour cream

1. In a food processor, combine the cilantro, scallions, jalapeños, and salt and process, stopping once to scrape down the sides of the work-bowl, until smooth.

2. In a bowl, whisk the sour cream until smooth and shiny. Stir in the puree and combine well. Taste, correct the seasoning, and refrigerate, covered, until serving time.

Jalapeño Shrimp Sauté
Serves 8 to 10

Tingling lips, buttery fingers, and succulent shrimp are the rewards for the messy work required in eating this zesty starter. In these days of Cajun madness, whole (heads-on) Gulf shrimp are increasingly available. Use them if you find them —they make the dish look and taste even better. Good as the shrimp are, though, the sauce approaches divine. Offer plenty of crusty bread for mopping up.

2 sticks (8 ounces) unsalted butter
2 medium fresh jalapeños, stemmed and minced
3 medium garlic cloves, peeled and minced
1½ pounds (about 36) unpeeled medium shrimp
 (see Note)
½ cup chopped scallions (including the green
 tops)
½ cup dry white wine
½ tablespoon Worcestershire sauce
1 teaspoon salt

 1. In a large skillet over medium heat, melt the butter. When it foams, add the jalapeños and garlic. Lower the heat and cook, stirring occasionally, for 5 minutes. Add the shrimp and scallions, raise the heat to high, and cook, tossing and stirring, until the shrimp turn a bright pink-orange and have curled, about 5 minutes.
 2. With a slotted spoon divide the shrimp among individual serving dishes (wide, shallow soup bowls or gratin dishes work best). Add the wine and Worcestershire sauce to the skillet, bring to a boil, and cook, stirring, for 3 minutes. Stir in the salt and pour equal amounts of the sauce over the shrimp in each dish. Serve at once.

▼▼▼▼NOTE: *Serve this in larger portions as a main course if you like, accompanied by white rice and a plain green vegetable. If you do locate whole shrimp, remember to double the weight you purchase to end up with the same number of shrimp.*

 # Guacamole

Makes about 4 cups, serving 6 to 8

The apparently insatiable American appetite for guacamole has resulted in an entire industry devoted to turning this fresh, simple preparation into a product, available as an acidic green paste that comes frozen in enormous cans. Once defrosted, it is mindlessly dolloped forth by food service personnel and just as mindlessly consumed by eager diners in restaurants from coast to coast. Such a product is waste-free, available year round, and the only element of human judgment involved is in selecting the right size can opener. This is not guacamole (it's barely food), but it is possible that if you have never tasted the real thing, you will eat it with relish. Here, to ruin for you forever the glories of frozen guacamole, is the recipe we serve at the restaurant. Certainly it's more trouble than opening a can, but if we can go through this twice a day, forty avocados at a time, you can manage it with four. The best—really, the *only*—avocado to use is the variety called Haas, those small, nubbly, black-skinned ones from California. They should be just ripe, giving slightly to thumb pressure. If there are no Haas avocados, or they are not perfectly ripe, make something else. If there

35

are no perfectly ripe tomatoes, omit them. If you can't find fresh cilantro, so be it: If the avocados are good, you won't miss the cilantro—much. Use pickled jalapeños if there are no fresh—not *as* good but okay. Dice the onions fine. Mash the avocados with a fork (for forty we use a restaurant-size potato masher) to produce a coarsely bumpy texture. Never, ever should guacamole be smooth. Above all, keep it simple (no sour cream, mayonnaise, cottage cheese, garlic salt, Tabasco sauce, lime juice, black olives, or carrot curls) and keep it fresh. Assemble the ingredients in advance and make the guacamole just before you want to eat it (it only takes 5 minutes) and never stash it in the refrigerator. There's no such thing as leftover guacamole—eat it or throw it out. It will be garbage long before tomorrow.

½ cup finely diced yellow onion
1 cup finely chopped clean fresh cilantro leaves
1 or 2 fresh jalapeños, stemmed and halved
½ teaspoon salt
4 perfectly ripe Haas avocados
6 perfectly ripe Italian plum tomatoes, seeded
    and diced
½ cup finely diced red onion

    1. In a blender or food processor, combine the yellow onion, *half* the cilantro, the jalapeños, and salt. Puree until smooth, scraping down the sides of the workbowl once.
    2. Halve, pit, and peel the avocados. In a medium bowl, using a fork, coarsely mash them. Stir in the puree from the processor; then stir in the diced tomatoes, red onion, and remaining cilantro. Taste and correct the seasoning—guacamole needs to be properly salted to really bring out the taste of the avocados—and use at once.

▼▼▼▼NOTE: *Actually the best kitchen appliance for pureeing the onion, cilantro, and jalapeño mixture is one of the new mini processors. I find mine indispensable when making guacamole at home. The unpleasant sour quality of frozen guacamole (and of some fresh versions) is due to enormous quantities of lime juice or some more dubious acid, included to prevent the guacamole from browning. I find such tartness completely masks the taste of the avocado, and is really unnecessary if your avocados are not overly ripe and if you use the guacamole at once. For storage beyond a few minutes, cover the guacamole with plastic wrap, pressing it down on the surface of the guacamole to prevent air from entering.*

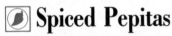 Spiced Pepitas

Makes 1 pound

These seasoned pumpkin seeds are a splendid light snack with drinks, whether the rest of the menu is Tex-Mex or not.

Corn oil
2 tablespoons mild, unseasoned chili powder
1 tablespoon ground cumin, from toasted seeds
1½ teaspoons coarse or Kosher salt
1½ teaspoons cayenne pepper, or to taste
½ teaspoon freshly ground black pepper
1 large egg white
Tabasco sauce to taste
1 pound (about 3½ cups) hulled raw pumpkin
seeds

37

1. Preheat the oven to 375°F. Brush a 9 × 13-inch jelly roll pan or other shallow baking pan lightly with corn oil.

2. In a small bowl, combine the chili powder, cumin, salt, and cayenne and black peppers.

3. In a medium mixing bowl, thoroughly whisk together the egg white and Tabasco sauce. Add the pumpkin seeds and stir until they are well coated with the egg white mixture. Working quickly, transfer the spice mixture to a small strainer. With one hand shake the spices over the wet pumpkin seeds while stirring them with the other.

4. Spread the coated pumpkin seeds on the prepared jelly roll pan and set on an oven rack in the middle of the oven. Bake, undisturbed, for 5 minutes. Stir the seeds, breaking up any clumps, and bake for another 10 minutes, stirring often, until they are puffed, crisp, and brown.

5. Transfer the pepitas immediately to a bowl, cool to room temperature, and store in an airtight tin or jar. The pepitas will keep for 10 days.

▼▼▼NOTE: *The best source for hulled raw pumpkin seeds is a health food store. You may also roast a combination of pumpkin seeds and unsalted, hulled peanuts, for a different taste. In humid weather, plan to eat the pepitas within 2 or 3 days.*

Chile con Queso

Makes about 2½ cups, serving 6 to 8

I have tasted complicated, fondue-like versions of this Tex-Mex classic. Made with first-rate aged cheeses and so on, they were edible but lacked the tacky charm of the original. If cooking with canned soups and processed cheeses fails to engage even your anthropologic curiosity, move on. If, on the other hand, a bowl of hot and cheesy "CCQ" and a basket of corn chips sets your middle-class motor to racing, this dip's for you.

1 can (28 ounces) Italian plum tomatoes, crushed and well drained
3 large jalapeños en escabeche, stemmed and minced
1 teaspoon dried oregano, preferably Mexican
2 cans (11 ounces each) condensed Cheddar Cheese soup
1 pound Velveeta, cut into 1-inch chunks
⅓ cup milk, approximately, optional
1 cup thinly sliced scallions (including the green tops)
1 teaspoon whole toasted cumin seeds

1. In a small heavy saucepan over low heat, combine the tomato pulp, jalapeños, and oregano. Cook, stirring constantly, until the mixture is fragrant and dry, about 5 minutes. Add the cheese soup and Velveeta to the pan and heat, stirring constantly, until the cheese has melted, about 15 minutes.
2. Thin the dip with the milk as desired, stir in the sliced scallions, and transfer to a serving bowl. Sprinkle with the cumin seeds and serve at once, accompanied by corn chips.

▼▼▼▼NOTE: *As a feeble bow to nutrition we also accompany the Chile con Queso with blanched broccoli spears. Texans know this is citified nonsense, and shove the broccoli aside; feel free to do as you wish. The dip can be prepared entirely in advance and refrigerated, covered, for up to 1 week. Reheat it in the top of a double boiler over simmering water or in a microwave oven just before serving.*

Nachos, Manhattan Chili Style
Serves 10 to 12

Giving a recipe for nachos is a little like giving one for peanut butter and jelly sandwiches—not only does everyone already know how, the process is so personal no two versions will ever be alike anyway. Still, our nachos are good, and different, and once you know our secret (we season our refried beans with chiles chipotles), you can—and probably will—proceed on your own.

2 cups (1 16-ounce can) refried beans, preferably
     imported from Mexico
4 to 6 finely chopped canned chiles chipotles,
     plus 2 to 3 tablespoons of sauce from the
     can, or to taste
100 unseasoned corn tortilla chips
12 ounces medium-sharp Cheddar cheese, grated
12 ounces Monterey Jack cheese, grated
Shredded romaine lettuce and sour cream, as
     garnish

1. Preheat the oven to 475°F. Position an oven rack in the upper third of the oven.

2. In a small bowl, stir together the refried beans, chopped chipotles, and chipotle sauce.

3. Spread each tortilla chip with about 1½ teaspoons of seasoned refried beans. Arrange the chips on a broiler-proof serving dish (using more than one dish or working in batches, if necessary). Sprinkle the two cheeses evenly over the nachos. Set the dish in the oven and bake until the nachos are hot and sizzling and any exposed edges are brown, about 4 minutes.

4. Garnish the dish with shredded lettuce and sour cream and serve at once.

▼▼▼NOTE: *The special smoky taste of chiles chipotles makes for unique nachos, but if they are unavailable (or you're a nacho traditionalist), just spread the tortilla chips with unseasoned refried beans, top each nacho with a slice of canned jalapeño en escabeche, sprinkle on the cheese, and broil away. The seasoned nacho base mixture, by the way, keeps for about 10 days, refrigerated, so that you can have nachos virtually on the spur of the moment—just like peanut butter and jelly sandwiches.*

THE CHILI RECIPES

However far afield our menu wanders, chili remains central. At any one time, we offer eight or nine on a regular basis, and the odd special shows up, too. There are as many chilies as there are cooks. This collection, by no means complete, contains representatives of the major chili styles from across the country. Somewhere in this chapter is *your* chili. Happy hunting!

Numero Uno

Serves 6 to 8

Chili-making requires a certain confidence. (Opening a chili restaurant requires even more.) This was my first chili recipe and easily became our favorite, hence its confident subtitle, "the best chili in the Universe." That said, I feel I must be honest and admit that it is also a fairly eccentric chili, though by no means universally so. The pork, tomato juice, and cinnamon all conspire to give it a slightly sweet quality, while the shock of just-cooked garlic, added right before serving, makes a sensational contrast. Easily our best seller.

¼ cup olive oil
2 large yellow onions, peeled and coarsely
    chopped (about 4 cups)
1½ pounds chili-grind beef

1½ pounds chili-grind pork
2 teaspoons salt
⅓ cup mild, unseasoned chili powder
3 tablespoons ground cumin, from toasted seeds
3 tablespoons dried oregano, preferably Mexican
3 tablespoons unsweetened cocoa powder (see
    Note)
2 tablespoons ground cinnamon
1½ teaspoons cayenne pepper, or to taste
4 cups tomato juice
3 cups beef stock or canned beef broth
8 medium garlic cloves, peeled and minced
2 to 3 tablespoons yellow cornmeal, as optional
    thickener
2 cans (16 ounces each) dark red kidney beans,
    drained and rinsed

1. In a large skillet over medium heat, warm the oil. Add the onions and cook, stirring occasionally, until very tender, about 20 minutes.

2. Meanwhile, in a 4½- to 5-quart heavy flameproof casserole or Dutch oven over medium heat, combine the beef and pork. Season with salt and cook, stirring often, until the meats have lost all pink color and are evenly crumbled, about 20 minutes.

3. Scrape the onions into the casserole with the meats. Stir in the chili powder, cumin, oregano, cocoa, cinnamon, and cayenne pepper and cook, stirring for 5 minutes. Stir in the tomato juice and beef stock and bring to a boil. Lower the heat and simmer, uncovered, for 1 hour.

4. Taste, correct the seasoning, and simmer for another 30 minutes, or until the chili is thickened to your liking. Stir in the garlic. To thicken the chili further, or to bind any surface fats, stir in the optional cornmeal. Stir in the beans and simmer for another 5 minutes.

▼▼▼NOTE: *Do not use a Dutch process cocoa—the regular sort is more flavorful. Originally the recipe called for 3 tablespoons of ground cinnamon, and though I have reduced that amount, I find that when I correct the seasoning, most of that lost tablespoon finds its way back into the chili. Proceed with caution, however, unless you are sure your guests or family are culinarily liberal: Some people can't abide any cinnamon in a savory dish. While the cayenne (and thus the heat of the chili) is a personal matter, the rather complicated balance of spices is thrown out of whack if the chili is too mild.*

The Real McCoy
Serves 4 to 6

This is the bean-less, tomato-less, classic Texas chili about which one hears so much (usually from Texans). If you thought a chili had to be complicated to be good, this recipe will be a revelation. For an even purer version, harking back to the days before commercially produced chili powder, substitute 1 cup Chili Paste (page 16) for the chili powder.

¼ cup rendered beef fat or olive oil
2 large yellow onions, peeled and coarsely
        chopped (about 4 cups)
8 medium garlic cloves, peeled and minced
4 pounds well-marbled beef chuck, trimmed of
        most external fat and cut into ½-inch cubes
1½ teaspoons salt
1 to 2 tablespoons olive oil
⅓ cup mild, unseasoned chili powder

2 tablespoons ground cumin, from toasted seeds
2 tablespoons dried oregano, preferably Mexican
1½ teaspoons cayenne pepper, or to taste
5 cups beef stock, prepared without salt, or 4
    cups canned beef broth diluted with 1 cup
    water
2 to 3 tablespoons yellow cornmeal, as optional
    thickener

1. In a large skillet over medium heat, warm the beef fat. Add the onions and garlic, lower the heat slightly, and cook, stirring once or twice, until very tender, about 20 minutes.

2. Meanwhile, set a 4½- to 5-quart heavy flameproof casserole or Dutch oven over medium heat. Add the beef, season with salt, and cook, uncovered, stirring often, until the meat has lost all pink color, about 20 minutes. (If the beef is very lean, it may stick slightly. Add olive oil.)

3. Scrape the onions and garlic into the casserole with the beef. Stir in the chili powder (or the paste, if you are using it), cumin, oregano, and cayenne pepper and cook, stirring, for 5 minutes. Stir in the beef stock and bring to a boil. Lower the heat and simmer, uncovered, stirring occasionally, for 1½ hours.

4. Taste, correct the seasoning, and add water if the chili is thickening too rapidly. Continue to simmer, stirring often, for another 30 minutes, or until the meat is tender and the chili is reduced to your liking.

5. To further thicken the chili, or to bind any surface fats, stir in the optional cornmeal and simmer the chili for another 5 minutes.

▼▼▼ NOTE: *This is one chili that deserves to be eaten plain, without a clutter of fixin's, at least the first time you prepare it.*

Texas Chain Gang Chili
Serves 6 to 8

Institutional chilies—those from the kitchens of schools or the armed forces—have an almost mythical reputation. Prisons in particular, it seems, have a knack for turning out the hot stuff —chili so good, in fact, ex-cons have reportedly committed crimes just to get back on line for another bowl. Herewith our version of the jail-house classic, and if we can do something toward reducing crime on the streets by printing it, well, we're glad to do so. Notice that the chili is very hot (cons can take it) and that it is unthickened. The combination of ground and cubed meat is particularly satisfying to eat.

¼ cup rendered bacon fat or olive oil
2 large yellow onions, peeled and coarsely
    chopped (about 4 cups)
8 medium garlic cloves, peeled and minced
8 fresh jalapeños, stemmed and minced
1½ pounds chili-grind beef
1½ pounds well-marbled beef chuck, trimmed of
    most external fat and cut into ½-inch cubes
2 teaspoons salt
5 tablespoons mild, unseasoned chili powder
2 tablespoons ground cumin, from toasted seeds
2 tablespoons dried oregano, preferably Mexican
2 teaspoons cayenne pepper, or to taste
1 can (28 ounces) Italian plum tomatoes, crushed
    and well drained
4 cups beef stock or canned beef broth
2 cans (16 ounces each) dark red kidney beans,
    rinsed and drained

1. In a large skillet over medium heat, warm the bacon fat. Add the onions, garlic, and jalapeños, lower the heat slightly, and cook, stirring once or twice, until very tender, about 20 minutes.

2. Meanwhile, set a 4½- to 5-quart heavy flameproof casserole or Dutch oven over medium heat. Add the chili-grind beef and cubed chuck, season with salt, and cook, uncovered, stirring often, until the meat is evenly crumbled and has lost all pink color, about 20 minutes.

3. Scrape the onion mixture into the casserole with the beef. Stir in the chili powder, cumin, oregano, and cayenne pepper and cook, stirring, for 5 minutes. Stir in the tomatoes and beef stock and bring to a boil. Lower the heat and simmer, uncovered, stirring occasionally, for 1½ hours.

4. Taste, correct the seasoning, and continue to simmer, stirring often, for another 30 minutes, or until the meat is tender and the chili is reduced to your liking. Stir in the kidney beans and simmer for another 5 minutes.

Abilene Choral Society and Music Guild Chili
Serves 6 to 8

In other words, a "gourmet" chili for tenderfeet and other genteel types. This tasty chili always surprises chili heads who think they only like it hot.

6 tablespoons olive oil
2 large yellow onions, peeled and coarsely chopped (about 4 cups)
3 large celery stalks, finely chopped
6 medium garlic cloves, peeled and minced
3 pounds chili-grind beef
2 teaspoons salt
⅓ cup mild, unseasoned chili powder
2 tablespoons ground cumin, from toasted seeds
1½ tablespoons dried basil
1 tablespoon dried oregano, preferably Mexican
½ teaspoon cayenne pepper, or to taste
1 can (35 ounces) Italian plum tomatoes, crushed and well drained
4 cups beef stock or canned beef broth
1½ cups hearty dry red wine
2 large sweet green peppers, stemmed, cored, and diced
2 large sweet red peppers, stemmed, cored, and diced
2 to 3 tablespoons yellow cornmeal, as optional thickener
2 cans (16 ounces each) dark red kidney beans, drained and rinsed

1. In a large skillet over medium heat, warm 3 tablespoons of the oil. Add the onions, celery, and garlic, lower the heat slightly, and cook, stir-

ring once or twice, until very tender, about 20 minutes.

2. Meanwhile, set a 4½- to 5-quart heavy flameproof casserole or Dutch oven over medium heat. Add the beef, season with salt, and cook, uncovered, stirring often, until the meat is evenly crumbled and has lost all pink color, about 20 minutes.

3. Scrape the onion mixture into the casserole with the beef. Stir in the chili powder, cumin, basil, oregano, and cayenne pepper and cook, stirring, for 5 minutes. Stir in the tomatoes, beef stock, and red wine and bring to a boil. Lower the heat and simmer, uncovered, stirring occasionally, for 1 hour.

4. Meanwhile, in a medium skillet, warm the remaining 3 tablespoons of oil over high heat. When it is very hot, add the diced green and red peppers and cook, tossing and stirring, for about 5 minutes, or until the peppers are lightly browned. Set them aside.

5. Taste the chili, correct the seasoning, and add the sautéed peppers. Continue to simmer, stirring often, for another 30 minutes, or until the meat is tender and the chili is reduced to your liking.

6. To further thicken the chili, or to bind any surface fats, stir in the optional cornmeal. Stir in the kidney beans and simmer for another 5 minutes, or until heated through.

▼▼▼ NOTE: *For a particularly rich and delicious chili, substitute chili-grind pork for half of the beef. Of all the chilies, this one seems to benefit the most from an overnight rest before serving.*

Green Chili with Pork
Serves 6 to 8

This is the "other" chili, the southwestern green chili rarely found east of Colorado. Of all the chili pilgrims who show up weary but hopeful on our doorstep, those who seek Green Chili seem to have traveled farther and longer than the others. The trip is worth it: Who says good chili has to be red?

¼ cup olive oil
2 large yellow onions, peeled and coarsely
    chopped (about 4 cups)
8 medium garlic cloves, peeled and minced
8 fresh jalapeños, stemmed and minced
3 carrots, peeled and sliced crosswise into
    ½-inch pieces
1½ tablespoons dried oregano, preferably
    Mexican
2½ to 3 pounds boneless pork shoulder, cut into
    ½-inch cubes
5 cups chicken stock or canned chicken broth
1 teaspoon salt
1 can (28 ounces) Italian plum tomatoes, crushed
    and well drained
1 potato, about 8 ounces, peeled and grated
12 large fresh poblano chiles (about 1½ pounds
    total weight), roasted and peeled (see Note),
    or 1 can (27 ounces) whole roasted mild
    green chiles, drained

1. In a 4½- to 5-quart heavy flameproof casserole or Dutch oven over medium heat, warm the oil. Add the onions, garlic, jalapeños, and carrots and cook, stirring once or twice, for 10 minutes. Stir in the oregano and the pork cubes and cook,

50

stirring occasionally, until the meat has lost all pink color, about 20 minutes.

2. Stir in the chicken stock, salt, the tomatoes, and the grated potato. Bring to a boil, lower the heat, partially cover, and cook, stirring occasionally, for 1½ hours.

3. Cut the chiles into ½-inch strips. Add them to the chili and cook, stirring often, for another 30 to 45 minutes, or until the pork is tender and the chili thickened to your liking. Taste, correct the seasoning, and simmer for another 5 minutes.

▼▼▼NOTE: *To roast poblanos, turn them in the open flame of a gas burner (or under a broiler) until thoroughly charred. Wrap the chiles in a paper bag as you roast them; when cool, rinse them under cool running water, rubbing off the burned skin with your fingers. Pat the chiles dry and stem them. Poblanos can range from bell pepper-like sweetness to quite hot. If the ultimate heat level of the chili is important to you, roast, peel, and taste one or two of your poblanos before beginning the chili. If they are very hot you may wish to omit the jalapeños. Canned, fire-roasted chiles are quite mild, and you will want to use them in conjunction with the jalapeños for a properly zesty chili.*

Three-Bean Vegetable Chili

Serves 8

"I hope you'll have a meatless chili," was a common request when we began work on the restaurant. More out of a sense of duty than with any real enthusiasm, I set out to do what I could and was surprised at the savory result. Making decent chili without meat mostly requires a lot of overcompensation. The notion of using bulgur to supply the "meaty" bulk comes from Jane Butel's charming *Chili Madness*, while the added garniture of three kinds of beans, corn, peppers, zucchini, tomatoes, scallions, and sour cream is based on the belief that too much of a good thing is a better thing. Note that this is a vegetable, rather than a vegetarian, chili, and, while I like it best made with chicken stock, it can be made with water instead. Omit the sour cream, too, and you have a cholesterol-free but entirely hearty, satisfying, and nutritious chili.

¾ cup medium or coarse bulgur (processed cracked wheat)
1 cup fresh orange juice
⅓ cup olive oil
2 large yellow onions, peeled and coarsely chopped (about 4 cups)
8 medium garlic cloves, peeled and minced
⅓ cup mild, unseasoned chili powder
3 tablespoons ground cumin, from toasted seeds
3 tablespoons dried oregano, preferably Mexican
1½ tablespoons dried thyme
1 to 2 teaspoons cayenne pepper, or to taste
¼ teaspoon ground cinnamon
1 can (35 ounces) Italian plum tomatoes, with their juice

3 cups chicken stock, canned chicken broth, or
    water
2 tablespoons salt
3 quarts water
½ pound fresh green beans, with ends trimmed,
    cut into 2-inch pieces
2 large sweet red peppers, stemmed, cored, and
    cut into ½-inch dice
1 package (10 ounces) frozen corn kernels,
    thawed and drained
1 can (16 ounces) dark red kidney beans, rinsed
    and drained
1 can (16 ounces) chick-peas (garbanzo beans),
    rinsed and drained
2 medium zucchini, scrubbed and coarsely
    shredded; 3 medium ripe tomatoes, seeded
    and diced; 1 bunch scallions, trimmed and
    sliced; 1 pint sour cream, as garnish

1. In a small bowl, combine the bulgur and
orange juice and let stand at room temperature,
stirring occasionally, while you prepare the rest of
the chili.

2. In a 5-quart heavy flameproof casserole or
Dutch oven over medium heat, warm the oil. Add
the onions and garlic, lower the heat slightly, and
cook, stirring, for 20 minutes, or until the vegetables are very tender. Stir in the chili powder,
cumin, oregano, thyme, cayenne pepper, and cinnamon and cook, stirring constantly, for 5 minutes.

3. Add the tomatoes, breaking them up with
your fingers, their juice, and chicken stock. Stir
in 1 tablespoon of salt and bring to a boil, skimming any scum that forms. Lower the heat, partially cover, and simmer, stirring once or twice,
for 25 minutes.

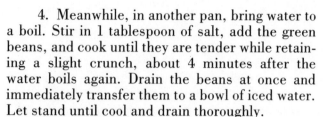

4. Meanwhile, in another pan, bring water to a boil. Stir in 1 tablespoon of salt, add the green beans, and cook until they are tender while retaining a slight crunch, about 4 minutes after the water boils again. Drain the beans at once and immediately transfer them to a bowl of iced water. Let stand until cool and drain thoroughly.

5. Uncover the chili, stir in the diced sweet peppers and cook, uncovered, stirring once or twice, for 20 minutes.

6. Stir in the bulgur and continue to cook, stirring occasionally, for 25 minutes, or until the chili has thickened considerably. Stir in the green beans, corn, kidney beans, and chick-peas. Taste, correct the seasonings, and simmer for another 5 minutes.

7. To serve, ladle the chili into bowls. Garnish with zucchini, tomatoes, scallions, and sour cream and serve at once.

▼▼▼▼NOTE: *This is another chili that can really use an overnight rest in the refrigerator to taste its best. For a change of pace that sounds offbeat but tastes surprisingly logical, try Francine's Vegetable Chili and Chèvre Gratin: Preheat the broiler. For each serving, spoon 1 cup hot Vegetable Chili into an individual gratin dish. Crumble 1½ to 2 ounces soft, mild goat cheese over the chili and broil for about 2 minutes, or until the chili is bubbling and the cheese is lightly browned. Garnish, or not, with zucchini et al. The best place to locate medium (sometimes labeled "coarse") bulgur, by the way, is a health food store. Supermarket bulgurs often include pilaf seasoning mixtures, which are inappropriate in this chili.*

Seafood Chili San Carlos
Serves 8

Nothing could be further from chili's landlocked traditions than this briny seafood stew. Nonetheless, the flavor is unmistakably that of chili, and the roll-your-sleeves-up-and-dig-in heartiness is totally authentic. As with any of the world's bouillabaisse-like seafood stews, using readily available fresh ingredients takes precedence over fidelity to the recipe. You might consider using a truly hearty fish, such as swordfish or tuna, and omitting the shellfish altogether. Crab would be a good addition, as would squid; or the chili could be made entirely with shrimp. Since the chili base must be made at least 24 hours in advance, and the seafood then cooks in minutes, this is perfect party fare. Serve it with a spicy California Gewürztraminer, such as those from Chateau St. Jean.

¼ cup olive oil
1 large yellow onion, peeled and coarsely
    chopped (about 2 cups)
2 large leeks (white part only), well cleaned and
    chopped
1 large celery stalk, chopped
8 medium garlic cloves, peeled and minced
2 tablespoons dried oregano, preferably Mexican
4½ teaspoons ground cumin, from toasted seeds
1 can (35 ounces) Italian plum tomatoes, with
    their juice
2 cups homemade fish stock or bottled clam juice
2 cups dry red wine
½ cup chili paste (see Note)
1 tablespoon salt
1 teaspoon cayenne pepper, or to taste

2 medium sweet red peppers, stemmed, cored,
and cut into ½-inch dice
2 medium sweet green peppers, stemmed, cored,
and cut into ½-inch dice
12 littleneck clams, scrubbed
12 mussels, scrubbed and debearded
1½ pounds scrod or other lean white fish fillets,
cut into 1-inch pieces
12 large shrimp, shelled and deveined but with
tails left on
¾ pound bay scallops
½ cup finely chopped clean fresh cilantro leaves

1. In a 4½- to 5-quart heavy flameproof casserole or Dutch oven, heat the oil. Add the onion, leeks, and celery, cover, and cook, stirring once or twice, for 20 minutes, or until the vegetables are very tender.

2. Add the garlic, oregano, and cumin, cover, and cook for 10 minutes, stirring occasionally.

3. Add the tomatoes, breaking them up with your fingers, their juice, fish stock, red wine, chili paste, salt, and cayenne pepper. Bring to a boil, skimming any scum that forms. Lower the heat, cover, and simmer, skimming and stirring occasionally, for 1 hour.

4. Stir in the sweet peppers and simmer, uncovered, for another 20 minutes. Cool to room temperature, cover, and refrigerate overnight.

5. Bring the chili base slowly to a boil, stirring often. Lower the heat so the chili simmers briskly. Taste and correct the seasoning. Add the clams and mussels, cover, and cook for 10 minutes, removing the shellfish as they open and arranging them in chili bowls. After 10 minutes, discard any that have not opened.

6. Stir in the scrod and shrimp, cover and simmer 1 minute. Add the scallops, cover, and simmer until the shrimp and scallops are just opaque and the scrod is beginning to flake, about 4 minutes.

7. Ladle the chili over shellfish in the bowls, dividing the shrimp evenly. Sprinkle each serving with cilantro.

▼▼▼NOTE: *Either homemade or commercial chili paste can be used in this recipe. If you use the chili paste recipe given in this book (page 16), omit the cayenne pepper from the chili—you won't need it.*

Lamb Chili on a Bed of Jalapeño Hominy

Serves 6 to 8

In Cincinnati, the Chili Capital of the World (more chili parlors per capita), the predominant chili style reflects the Greek and Bulgarian origins of the founders of the city's two leading parlors. The subtle, Middle-Eastern spicing goes particularly well with the lamb in this chili, although we serve it on a bed of all-American hominy with jalapēnos.

¼ cup olive oil
2 large yellow onions, peeled and coarsely
      chopped (about 4 cups)
6 medium garlic cloves, peeled and minced
3 pounds lean chili-grind lamb
2 teaspoons salt

⅓ cup mild, unseasoned chili powder
2 tablespoons ground cumin, from toasted seeds
1 tablespoon dried oregano, preferably Mexican
1 tablespoon freshly ground black pepper
2 teaspoons ground cinnamon
1½ teaspoons dried thyme
1 teaspoon ground ginger
1 teaspoon ground allspice
1 teaspoon powdered mustard
1 can (28 ounces) Italian plum tomatoes, crushed
    and well drained
4 cups beef stock or canned beef broth
2 to 3 tablespoons yellow cornmeal, as optional
    thickener
6 tablespoons unsalted butter
2 fresh jalapeños, or to taste, stemmed and
    minced
2 cans (27 ounces each) white or yellow hominy
    (or 1 can of each), drained
Thin wedges of unpeeled avocado and tomato
    and rings of red onion, as garnish

1. In a large skillet over medium heat, warm the oil. Add the onions and garlic, lower the heat slightly, and cook, stirring once or twice, until very tender, about 20 minutes.

2. Meanwhile, set a 4½- to 5-quart heavy flameproof casserole or Dutch oven over medium heat. Add the lamb, season with salt, and cook, uncovered, stirring often, until the meat is evenly crumbled and has lost all pink color, about 20 minutes.

3. Scrape the onions and garlic into the casserole with the lamb. Stir in the chili powder, cumin, oregano, black pepper, cinnamon, thyme, ginger, allspice, and mustard and cook, stirring, for 5 minutes. Stir in the tomatoes and beef stock and bring to a boil. Lower the heat and simmer, uncovered, stirring occasionally, for 1½ hours.

4. Taste, correct the seasoning, and add an additional ½ cup or so of water if the chili seems too thick. Continue to simmer, stirring often, for another 30 minutes, or until the meat is tender and the chili is reduced to your liking.

5. To further thicken the chili, or to bind any surface fats, stir in the optional cornmeal and simmer for another 5 minutes.

6. While the chili cooks, prepare the hominy. In a medium skillet over moderate heat, melt the butter. When it foams, add the jalapeños. Turn the heat to very low, cover the skillet, and cook, stirring once or twice, for 10 minutes. Do not allow the jalapeños to brown. Uncover, raise the heat, and add the drained hominy. Cook, stirring and tossing, until heated through, 3 to 5 minutes.

7. To serve, divide the hominy among bowls and ladle the chili over it, leaving a visible border of hominy around the edges of the bowls. Garnish and serve at once.

High Plains Buffalo Chili
Serves 8

This chuck-wagon chili springs entirely from my imagination, but is not, I hope, too far from how it might have been many years ago. The trail-drive chef, gifted with a fresh buffalo or two, improvises a tasty chili dinner using the morning's bacon drippings and some dried pinto beans, and tosses in a generous tot of leftover cowboy coffee to give the thing a little kick. The result, despite the contrary nature of the main ingredients, is superb chili. Buffalo (which is lean and flavorful) is increasingly available again by mail, but if your hunter comes home empty-handed, just substitute beef chuck.

2 cups dry pinto beans, sorted and soaked for 24
    hours in cold water to cover
1 tablespoon salt
6 tablespoons bacon drippings
2 large yellow onions, peeled and coarsely
    chopped (about 4 cups)
8 medium garlic cloves, peeled and minced
4 pounds boneless buffalo chuck, trimmed and
    cut into ½-inch cubes
⅓ cup mild, unseasoned chili powder
2 tablespoons ground cumin, from toasted seeds
2 tablespoons dried oregano, preferably Mexican
1 tablespoon sweet paprika, preferably imported
    Hungarian
1½ teaspoons cayenne pepper, or to taste
3 cups tomato juice
2½ cups beef stock or canned beef broth
1 cup strong black coffee

    1. Drain the beans. Transfer them to a 4-quart pan, add cold water to cover them by at least

3 inches, and set over medium heat. Bring to a boil, skimming any scum that forms. Lower the heat, partially cover, and simmer the beans, stirring occasionally, for 45 minutes. Stir in salt and continue to cook the beans, partially covered, until they are just tender while still remaining firm and holding their shape, about 30 minutes. Drain and reserve.

2. In a large skillet over medium heat, melt half the bacon drippings. Add the onions and garlic, lower the heat slightly, and cook, stirring once or twice, until very tender, about 20 minutes.

3. Meanwhile, set a 4½- to 5-quart heavy flameproof casserole or Dutch oven over medium heat. Melt the remaining bacon drippings, add the buffalo meat, and cook, uncovered, stirring occasionally, until the meat has lost all pink color, about 20 minutes.

4. Scrape the onions and garlic into the casserole with the meat. Stir in the chili powder, cumin, oregano, paprika, and cayenne pepper and cook, stirring, for 5 minutes. Add the tomato juice, beef stock, and coffee and bring to a boil. Lower the heat and simmer the chili for 1½ hours, stirring occasionally.

5. Taste, correct the seasoning, and simmer for another 30 to 45 minutes, or until the meat is tender (buffalo will take longer than beef). If the chili becomes too thick before the meat is tender, add ½ cup water and continue to cook. Stir the drained beans into the chili when you estimate it has about 15 minutes of cooking time left.

▼▼▼ NOTE: *See Mail-Order Sources (page 115) for a mail-order source for buffalo. This chili is particularly delicious made with your own chili paste instead of the powder—see page 16. An excellent fixin' with this flavor combination is sour cream.*

Venison Chili with Black Beans, Orange Peel, and Sour Cream

Serves 8

Venison may well have been the original chili meat, and it remains a favorite of serious chili cooks both for its resilient texture, which holds up well under long simmering, and for its rich flavor. This opulent chili—a sometime special at the restaurant—could well be the centerpiece of a black-tie-and-champagne buffet.

½ pound bacon, finely chopped
2 tablespoons vegetable oil
3 pounds boneless venison, trimmed of all sinew
    and cut into ½-inch cubes
2 large yellow onions, peeled and coarsely
    chopped (about 4 cups)
8 medium garlic cloves, peeled and minced
⅓ cup mild, unseasoned chili powder
3 tablespoons ground cumin, from toasted seeds
1½ tablespoons dried oregano, preferably
    Mexican
¾ teaspoon cayenne pepper, or to taste
6 cups beef stock or canned beef broth
Salt
2 to 3 tablespoons yellow cornmeal, as optional
    thickener
2 cans (16 ounces each) black beans, rinsed and
    drained
Sour cream, orange peel, and minced clean fresh
    cilantro leaves, as garnish

1. In a 4½ to 5-quart heavy flameproof casserole or Dutch oven, combine the bacon and oil. Set the casserole over medium heat and cook, stir-

ring once or twice, until the bacon is crisp and has rendered its fat, 15 to 20 minutes. With a slotted spoon remove the bacon and drain it on paper towels. Pour half the rendered fat into a large skillet and set it aside.

2. Return the casserole to medium heat. Add the venison and cook, uncovered, stirring often, until the meat loses all red color, about 20 minutes.

3. Meanwhile, set the skillet over medium heat. Add the onions and garlic, lower the heat slightly, and cook, stirring once or twice, until very tender, about 20 minutes.

4. Scrape the onions and garlic into the casserole with the venison. Stir in the chili powder, cumin, oregano, and cayenne pepper and cook, stirring, for 5 minutes. Stir in the beef stock and the reserved bacon and bring to a boil. Lower the heat and simmer, uncovered, stirring occasionally, for 1½ hours.

5. Taste and correct the seasoning, adding salt if needed and water if the chili is thickening too rapidly. Continue to simmer, stirring often, for another 30 to 45 minutes, or until the meat is tender and the chili is reduced to your liking.

6. To further thicken the chili, or to bind any surface fats, stir in the optional cornmeal. Stir in the black beans and simmer for another 5 minutes, or until the beans are heated through.

7. To serve, ladle into bowls and garnish each serving with a dollop of sour cream and a sprinkling of orange peel and cilantro.

▼▼▼ NOTE: *See Mail-Order Sources (page 115) for a mail-order source for venison. Lean diced lamb or even beef can be substituted here. Use a zester to remove the orange peel in long, thin ornamental strands. Avoid salting the chili until near the end of the cooking time.*

OTHER SOUTHWESTERN FAVORITES, MANHATTAN CHILI STYLE

Some of the dishes in this chapter are truly authentic—primitive and powerful as only the food of a harsh land like the American Southwest can be. But our restaurant is located in New York, not Santa Fe, and along the way some very authentic dishes have picked up some decidedly Big Apple modifications. Taken collectively, both sorts of recipes represent some of the oldest and some of the newest approaches to what we call southwestern cooking.

Chicken Chili Fricassee with Vegetables
Serves 8

I can hear the shouting in San Antonio already, but those more concerned with something good to eat and less concerned with what is and what isn't properly chili will find this colorful skillet of food quite delicious. Make it a day in advance, if you wish, reserving only the cilantro and stirring it in just before serving. Accompany the fricassee, in wide shallow bowls, with white rice.

2 chickens (2½ to 3 pounds each), quartered
6 tablespoons olive oil
Salt
Freshly ground black pepper

2 large yellow onions, peeled and finely chopped
(about 4 cups)
6 medium garlic cloves, peeled and minced
5 tablespoons mild, unseasoned chili powder
2 tablespoons ground cumin, from toasted seeds
1½ tablespoons dried oregano, preferably
Mexican
½ teaspoon cayenne pepper, or to taste
1 can (35 ounces) Italian plum tomatoes, crushed
and well drained
2 cups chicken stock or canned chicken broth
1 cup Zinfandel or other hearty red wine
1 sweet red pepper, stemmed, cored, and cut
into thick julienne
1 sweet green pepper, stemmed, cored, and cut
into thick julienne
2 medium zucchini, scrubbed and cut into
½-inch dice
1 package (10 ounces) frozen corn kernels,
thawed and drained
1 cup finely chopped clean fresh cilantro leaves

1. Pat the chicken pieces dry with paper towels. In a large, deep skillet or wide, flameproof casserole, heat 4 tablespoons of the oil until very hot. Add half the chicken skin side down and lower the heat slightly. Season with salt and pepper and cook, turning once or twice, until lightly browned, about 10 minutes. With tongs, transfer the chicken to a bowl and reserve it. Repeat with the remaining chicken.

2. Turn the heat to low and add the onions and garlic to the pan. Partially cover and cook, stirring once or twice, until very tender, about 20 minutes.

3. Add the chili powder, cumin, oregano, and cayenne pepper and cook, stirring, for 5 minutes. Add the tomatoes, chicken stock, and wine. Raise heat and bring the mixture to a boil; then

65

lower the heat slightly and simmer, partially covered, for 30 minutes.

4. Return the chicken, along with any juices accumulated in the bowl, to the skillet. Cover tightly and simmer, turning once or twice, until the chicken is very tender, about 40 minutes.

5. Meanwhile, heat the remaining 2 tablespoons of oil in a medium skillet until very hot. Add red and green peppers and diced zucchini, lower the heat slightly, and season with salt and pepper. Cook, stirring and tossing, until the vegetables are lightly browned, about 10 minutes. Remove the skillet from the heat, stir in the corn, and set the vegetable mixture aside.

6. When the chicken is tender, transfer it with tongs to a bowl and reserve. Cool the braising mixture slightly; then puree in a food processor, in batches, or force through the fine blade of a food mill. Wipe out the skillet with paper towels and then return the puree to it.

7. Set the skillet over medium heat and bring the puree to a boil; then lower the heat slightly and simmer briskly, stirring often, for 15 minutes, or until the mixture is slightly reduced and thickened.

8. Taste and correct the seasoning. Add the sautéed vegetables to the skillet and simmer, uncovered, for 5 minutes. Return the chicken to the skillet and simmer, basting frequently with the chili mixture, for another 5 minutes, or until the chicken is heated through. Stir in the cilantro and serve immediately.

▼▼▼ NOTE: *A handful of imported black olives, either tiny Niçoise or larger Calamatas, makes a colorful addition to the fricassee. Add them when you return the chicken to the skillet for its final warming.*

Carnitas Salad

Serves 6 to 8

Carnitas—"little meats"—are a popular Mexican snack or quick meal of crisp nuggets of warm pork rolled up in flour tortillas and slathered with salsa or guacamole, or both. The pairings of cool/hot, crisp/soft, and bland/spicy make for wonderful eating, an effect I hope to capture with this very modern main-course salad. Arranged on a large platter and accompanied by cool white wine and crusty French bread (or warm flour tortillas) it makes a splendid summer supper.

3 pounds boneless pork, cut into ½-inch cubes
Salt
⅔ cup olive oil, approximately
1½ pounds small new potatoes, scrubbed
1 pound fresh green beans, with ends trimmed
2 large heads romaine lettuce
1 large ripe avocado, preferably Haas, pitted and
    cut into eighths
1½ cups diced tomato (from 3 large ripe
    tomatoes, about 1 pound total weight)
¼ cup good-quality red wine vinegar
¾ cup finely chopped clean fresh cilantro leaves
1 medium red onion, peeled and sliced into thin
    rings

    1. In a large, deep skillet or wide, flameproof casserole, combine the pork, 1½ teaspoons of salt, and 5 cups of cold water. Set over medium heat and bring to a boil, skimming any scum that forms. Lower the heat and simmer, uncovered, stirring once or twice, until all the water has evaporated from the skillet—about 1 hour. The pork should be tender; if not, add an additional cup of

water and simmer until it has evaporated and the pork is tender. The pork cubes will begin to brown in their rendered fat. Stir often and add 1 to 2 tablespoons of olive oil to the skillet if the meat sticks. The carnitas are done when they are crisp and thoroughly brown, 10 to 15 minutes after they begin to sizzle. Remove from the heat and cover to keep warm. (The carnitas can be prepared several hours in advance of serving. Rewarm them before proceeding.)

2. Meanwhile, halve the potatoes and put them into a medium saucepan. Cover them with cold water and stir in 1 tablespoon of salt. Set the pan over medium heat and bring to a boil. Lower the heat slightly and cook the potatoes until they are just tender, 8 to 10 minutes from when the water reaches the boil. Drain them and cool to room temperature.

3. Bring a second pan of water to a boil. Stir in 1 tablespoon of salt and add the green beans. Cook, uncovered, stirring once or twice, until the beans are just tender, about 5 minutes. Fill a bowl with cold water, add a tray of ice cubes, and, when the beans are ready, drain them and immediately plunge them into the iced water. Let stand until cool; then drain well.

4. Separate the heads of romaine into leaves, wash, and pat dry with paper towels. Reserve the dark outer leaves for another use. Line a large platter with the yellow inner leaves of romaine. Mound the potatoes at one end of the platter. Arrange the beans in a mound at the other end. Spoon the warm carnitas into the center of the platter and garnish with the avocado slices.

5. In a small skillet, combine the diced tomatoes and ½ cup of olive oil. Set over medium heat and cook, stirring, until the tomatoes are hot, 3 or 4 minutes. Stir in ½ teaspoon of salt, the vinegar, and the cilantro. Raise the heat, bring the

dressing just to the boil, and immediately spoon it over the salad. Garnish with the red onion rings and serve immediately, offering a pepper mill at the table.

▼▼▼NOTE: *Trimming and boning a 5- to 6-pound pork shoulder roast is really the only satisfactory way of arriving at the necessary 3 pounds of ½-inch cubes. Whether you do it yourself or pay the butcher to is a personal matter. Don't be tempted to buy something easier to deal with, such as a boneless loin roast, because it will be too lean and the carnitas unpleasantly dry.*

Chicken Salad with Salsa Mayonnaise

Serves 8

This chicken salad, tossed with a tangy salsa-inspired mayonnaise and piled high on a crisp corn tortilla, is one of our most popular non-chili entrées, both summer and winter.

Oil for frying
8 corn tortillas (5 to 6 inches in diameter)
3½ pounds (about 6) boneless chicken breasts
1 tablespoon salt
Salsa Mayonnaise (recipe follows)
3 celery stalks, trimmed and cut on the diagonal
    ½-inch thick
5 scallions (including the green tops), sliced
3 cups Guacamole (page 35)
8 cups finely shredded romaine lettuce (most of a
    good-size head)
½ cup Salsa Fresca (page 30)

1. Pour enough vegetable oil into a small skillet to make a ½-inch layer. Heat the oil over medium heat until hot. Using tongs, add the tortillas one at a time to the oil. Fry them until crisp, about 30 seconds, turning them once. Drain on paper towels.

2. In a skillet large enough to hold them in a single layer (or in two skillets), cover the chicken breasts with cold water. Stir in salt and set over medium heat. Poach the chicken for 20 minutes, turning the breasts at the halfway point (the water will probably just reach a simmer at the end of 20 minutes). Remove the skillet from the heat and let the chicken breasts stand, uncovered, in the poaching liquid until cool.

3. Drain the chicken. Cut away the central cartilege and any fatty or tough spots and tear the chicken into bite-size pieces.

4. In a medium bowl, toss the chicken with the Salsa Mayonnaise, celery, and scallions. Taste and correct the seasoning.

5. To serve the salad, spread each corn tortilla evenly with guacamole. Spread shredded lettuce over the guacamole, dividing evenly. Mound the chicken salad on the lettuce. Top each portion with 2 tablespoons of Salsa Fresca.

▼▼▼NOTE: *Having fresh guacamole and salsa on hand is a great luxury and we tend to use them lavishly. Those at home, however, who would like to make this salad without first having to make guacamole and salsa can still produce delicious fare. Omit the guacamole. Peel and pit 2 ripe Haas avocados. Cut them into ½-inch chunks and toss them with the chicken, mayonnaise, celery, and scallions. Omit the salsa and garnish the salad with diced ripe tomato.*

Salsa Mayonnaise
Makes 2½ cups

This luscious orange mayonnaise is also good with crudités or cold poached shrimp or other seafood. Adjust the spiciness to suit the occasion.

3 large egg yolks
¼ cup fresh lime juice
1½ teaspoons salt
¼ cup chili paste (see Note)
1 can (14 ounces) Italian plum tomatoes, crushed
    and well drained (about ⅓ cup pulp)
1 to 3 jalapeños en escabeche, stemmed
1 cup corn oil
1 cup good-quality olive oil

    1. In a food processor, combine the egg yolks, lime juice, salt, chili paste, crushed tomatoes, and pickled jalapeños. Process until smooth.
    2. With the motor running, dribble in the corn and olive oils in a quick steady stream. Scrape down the sides of the workbowl. Taste and correct the seasoning. Reprocess to blend. Transfer the mayonnaise to a bowl, cover, and refrigerate until ready to use.

▼▼▼NOTE: *You must use chili paste in this recipe, although it can be the commercially produced version or your own. If you follow the chili paste recipe given on page 16 exactly, be warned that the mayonnaise can be quite picante. You might then want to omit the jalapeños en escabeche.*

Chilied Lamb Shanks
Serves 3 to 6

The natural affinity between lamb and chili is exploited again in this hearty dish of braised lamb shanks. As with other tough cuts of "working" muscle, the shank, after a slow, moist simmer, produces tender, succulent meat and a ravishingly rich sauce. Serve it with steamed rice tossed with well-drained canned black beans and a tart green salad. (One shank per person *ought* to be enough, but somehow, when I serve this, it never is.)

½ cup olive oil
6 lamb shanks (about ¾ pound each)
Salt
Freshly ground black pepper
2 large yellow onions, peeled and coarsely
    chopped (about 4 cups)
8 medium garlic cloves, peeled and minced
⅓ cup mild, unseasoned chili powder
3 tablespoons ground cumin, from toasted seeds
3 tablespoons dried oregano, preferably Mexican
2 teaspoons cayenne pepper, or to taste
1 can (14 ounces) Italian plum tomatoes, with
    their juice
1 bottle (12 ounces) dark beer
1½ cups beef stock or canned beef broth

1. Preheat the oven to 350°F. In a 5-quart flameproof casserole or Dutch oven over medium heat, warm ¼ cup of the oil. When it is very hot, add half the lamb shanks. Season with salt and pepper and cook, turning often, until well browned on all sides, about 15 minutes. Transfer the shanks to a plate and reserve. Repeat with the remaining shanks. Discard the fat from pan.

2. Return the pan to medium heat. Add the remaining oil and, when it is hot, add the onions and garlic. Lower the heat slightly, cover, and cook, stirring once or twice, until tender and translucent, about 15 minutes. Uncover, stir in the chili powder, cumin, oregano, and cayenne pepper and cook, stirring constantly, for 5 minutes. Stir in the tomatoes, crushing them well with your fingers, their juice, the beer, beef stock, and 2 teaspoons of salt. Add the lamb shanks (the pan will be crowded) and bring to a boil. Cover and set on an oven rack in the middle of the oven.

3. Bake for 45 minutes, stirring and rearranging the shanks in the braising liquid once or twice. Uncover and bake for another 30 to 45 minutes, or until the shanks are very tender.

4. Remove the shanks from the braising liquid and keep them warm. Pour the liquid through a strainer set over a bowl, pressing hard on the solids with the back of a spoon to extract all juices. Discard the solids. Wipe out the pan with paper towels. Return the liquid to the pan, set it over high heat, and bring to a boil. Lower the heat slightly and cook briskly, skimming any surface fats or other impurities, until the sauce is reduced by one-third, about 15 minutes.

5. Taste and correct the seasoning. Return the shanks to the pan and turn them in the sauce, basting thoroughly, until the shanks are hot, 3 to 5 minutes. Serve at once.

Fajitas of Grilled Pork with Chiles Chipotles

6 to 8 servings

On my first trip to Houston, a flying 24-hour auto-graph junket, I was eager to ask local foodies about their favorite places for chili. Unfortunately, all they wanted to talk about was fajitas, the finger food of thin-sliced steak folded up into tortillas that had taken the city by storm. Eventually I, too, was won over by the primitive messiness of this snack food. Now fajitas have become Tex-Mex staples, rolled out as new items by fast-food chains and appearing on menus even in New York, where all Tex-Mex change occurs slowly, if at all. Skirt steak is traditional (if you can get your butcher to part with any), but pork is delicious, too.

1 can (35 ounces) Italian plum tomatoes, with
    their juice
4 canned chiles chipotles (page 18), finely
    minced, with 1 to 2 tablespoons sauce from
    the can, or to taste
1 teaspoon salt
5 scallions (including the green tops), thickly
    sliced
1 cup finely chopped clean fresh cilantro leaves
1 2½- to 3-pound boneless pork loin roast,
    trimmed of surface fat
¼ cup olive oil
4½ tablespoons fresh lime juice
2 teaspoons ground cumin, from toasted seeds
2 large garlic cloves, crushed
2 large ripe avocados, preferably Haas
6 to 8 flour tortillas (8 to 10 inches in diameter)

1. In a small saucepan, combine the tomatoes, breaking them up with your fingers, their juice, the chipotles, their sauce, and the salt. Set over medium heat and bring to a boil. Lower the heat to a simmer and cook, uncovered, stirring occasionally, until thick, about 40 minutes.

2. Stir in the scallions and simmer for another 5 minutes. Remove from the heat and cool to room temperature. Stir in the cilantro, cover, and refrigerate. (The sauce can be prepared 24 hours in advance of serving. Bring it to room temperature before proceeding.)

3. Remove the thin strip of fatty meat that runs along one side of the pork loin and reserve it for another use. (It makes good chili meat.) Slice the pork into 18 to 24 ¼-inch pieces. In a small bowl, blend the oil, 3 tablespoons of the lime juice, the cumin, and garlic. Dip each slice of pork into the mixture; then put them into a medium bowl. Pour any remaining marinade over the pork and let stand at room temperature for 1 hour, stirring twice.

4. Prepare an outdoor grill, heating the coals until they are white. Position a rack 6 inches above the coals. Arrange the pork on the rack and grill until lightly browned and no pink remains, about 3 minutes per side.

5. Peel and coarsely mash the avocados. Stir in the remaining lime juice. Warm the tortillas in a low oven or on the grill.

6. To serve, set out the fajitas, warmed tortillas, avocado puree, and chipotle sauce. Lay a tortilla on a plate. Spread about ¼ cup of the avocado puree down the center of the tortilla. Arrange 2 or 3 slices of pork over the avocado. Top with 1 or 2 tablespoons of sauce. Fold the bottom edge of the tortilla about one quarter of the way up, fold in both sides and eat the fajitas from your hands.

Chicken Tortilla Pie

6 servings

When the critics recommend something besides one of our chilies, they're usually talking about this Mexican-inspired casserole of chicken layered with flour tortillas, refried beans, and cheese. It's a good company dish, because everything not only *can* but *should* be done a day ahead.

3 pounds chicken dark meat quarters (about
      6 leg/thigh combination pieces)
1 medium yellow onion, quartered but unpeeled
1 unpeeled carrot, chopped
Salt
½ cup sour cream
8 ounces medium-sharp Cheddar cheese
8 ounces Monterey Jack cheese
Rich Red Chile Sauce (recipe follows)
6 10-inch slightly stale flour tortillas
1 cup refried beans at room temperature
Finely shredded romaine lettuce, sliced scallions,
      and additional sour cream, as garnish

    1. In a 4½- to 5-quart saucepan, cover the chicken, onion, and carrot with cold water. Stir in 1½ teaspoons of salt, set over medium heat, and bring just to a boil. Lower the heat slightly, skim any scum that forms, and simmer, uncovered, until the meat is falling-off-the-bones tender, about 45 minutes. Remove from the heat and cool the chicken in the stock to room temperature.

    2. Pour the stock through a strainer set over a bowl. Discard the onion and carrot. Reserve the stock for use in the Chili Sauce below. Remove the skin from the chicken and discard it. Tear the meat from the bones and shred it coarsely.

3. In a medium bowl, combine the shredded meat with the sour cream and set it aside. Coarsely grate the cheeses and, in a medium bowl, toss to combine them. Set aside. Preheat the oven to 350°F.

4. In a small saucepan over low heat, warm 2 cups of the Rich Red Chili Sauce. With a pastry brush lightly paint the bottom of a 10-inch spring-form pan with 2 tablespoons of the sauce. Evenly spread a tortilla with ⅓ cup of refried beans and place the tortilla, beans up, in the bottom of the springform. Sprinkle the beans with one quarter of the grated cheese; then drizzle with ¼ cup of warm sauce. Add a second tortilla to the pan. (Avoid actually pressing the tortilla onto the previous layer or the pie will be too flat.) Spread half the shredded chicken over the second tortilla. Drizzle the chicken with ¼ cup of sauce. Spread the third tortilla with ⅓ cup refried beans and place in the pan. Sprinkle with one third of the remaining cheese and drizzle with ¼ cup of sauce. Place the fourth tortilla in the pan, spread it with the remaining chicken, and drizzle with ¼ cup of sauce. Spread the fifth tortilla with the remaining refried beans and place in the pan. Sprinkle with half the remaining cheese and drizzle with ¼ cup of sauce. Add the last tortilla to the pan. Drizzle it with ¼ cup of sauce and sprinkle with the remaining cheese.

5. Bake, uncovered, on the center rack of the oven for 30 minutes. Cool completely; then cover and refrigerate overnight.

6. To serve the pie, preheat the oven to 375°F. Run a thin sharp knife around the edge of the pan and release and remove the sides. Cut the pie into 6 wedges. Transfer the wedges to a baking sheet, spacing them well apart, and wrap tightly with aluminum foil. Bake until heated through, 30 to 40 minutes.

7. Meanwhile, warm the remaining sauce over medium-low heat, stirring once or twice, until it is simmering. With a spatula, transfer the wedges of the pie to plates. Spoon ⅓ to ½ cup heated sauce over and around each wedge. Garnish with shredded romaine, sliced scallions, and a generous dollop of sour cream. Serve at once.

▼▼▼NOTE: *If the tortillas are fresh, spread them on a work surface in a single layer and let them stand, uncovered, for about 1 hour, or until the edges curl and crack slightly. Good-quality canned refried beans are an acceptable convenience in this recipe. Select a brand containing only beans, lard, and salt—the best are usually imported from Mexico.*

Rich Red Chile Sauce
Makes about 8 cups

Because canned red chili or enchilada sauces are so dreadful, and making one's own at home is so easy and the results so good, there is really no excuse for not doing so. Our version is delicious over eggs and enchiladas, or as a braising medium for browned chicken quarters, and it is indispensable when making Chicken Tortilla Pie.

⅔ cup olive oil
1 large yellow onion, peeled and finely chopped
    (about 2 cups)
6 medium garlic cloves, peeled and minced
⅔ cup unbleached all-purpose flour, measured by
    scooping into dry measure cups and
    sweeping level
⅔ cup mild, unseasoned chili powder, or 2 cups,
    approximately, commercial or homemade
    chili paste (page 16)

2 tablespoons ground cumin, from toasted seeds
2 tablespoons dried oregano, preferably Mexican
2 tablespoons unsweetened cocoa, *not* Dutch
    process
1 to 1½ teaspoons cayenne pepper, or to taste
Chicken stock reserved from poached legs, or
    8 cups canned chicken broth
2½ teaspoons salt

1. In a heavy 4-quart saucepan over medium heat, warm the olive oil. When hot stir in the onion and garlic, turn the heat to low, and cook, covered, stirring once or twice, until the onion is very tender and lightly colored, about 20 minutes.

2. In a small bowl, sift together the flour, chili powder, cumin, oregano, cocoa, and cayenne pepper. Gradually stir the flour-and-spice mixture into the saucepan. Cook over low heat, stirring and mashing constantly, for 3 minutes. Do not allow the mixture to scorch.

3. Add enough water to the chicken leg stock to equal 8 cups. (Or you may use canned chicken broth.) Slowly whisk the stock into the flour mixture. Stir in salt. Raise the heat and bring to a boil; then lower the heat to medium and simmer briskly, uncovered, stirring occasionally, until reduced to 8 cups, 30 to 40 minutes.

4. Taste for salt and add additional cayenne pepper if you would like the sauce spicier. (Plain sauce will taste slightly bitter; this is as it should be. For a more accurate impression of how the sauce will taste in the finished dish, dip a piece of tortilla or bread into the sauce.) Cool to room temperature, cover, and refrigerate until ready to use.

▼▼▼NOTE: *If you are using chili paste, either a commercially available brand or your own home-made paste, eliminate the chili powder. Whisk the chili paste into the sauce just after you whisk in the stock.*

Crab Enchiladas Suiza
Serves 6

This is not the gourmet affectation that you may, at first, think it is. Rather it is in the tradition of the so-called Swiss enchiladas—whose sauce in some way incorporates cream—served throughout the Southwest, admittedly often at restaurants with gourmet aspirations. Rich and on the mild side, the enchiladas are typically filled with turkey, chicken, shrimp, or crab. Assembling enchiladas is always a messy business, but they are almost a pleasure when served in flat stacks, instead of being filled and rolled. Serve this as an offbeat but elegant supper or as a Tex-Mex brunch, accompanied by Calico Corn Muffins (page 95) and chilled fresh pineapple.

3 cups heavy cream
8 ounces Monterey Jack cheese, grated
8 ounces medium-sharp Cheddar cheese, grated
½ teaspoon salt
Freshly ground black pepper
4 tablespoons unsalted butter
1 large sweet red pepper, stemmed, cored, and
 cut into ¼-inch dice
2 medium fresh jalapeños, stemmed and minced
1 medium garlic clove, peeled and minced
1 cup chopped scallions (including the green
 tops)
1½ teaspoons dried oregano, preferably Mexican
1 can (14 ounces) Italian plum tomatoes, crushed
 and well drained (about ⅓ cup pulp)
1 pound lump crabmeat, picked over
18 corn tortillas (5 to 6 inches in diameter)
Finely shredded inner leaves of romaine,
 additional chopped scallions and thin,
 unpeeled slices of Haas avocado, as garnish

1. In a medium saucepan over medium heat, bring the cream to a boil. Lower the heat slightly and simmer the cream briskly, uncovered, for 15 minutes. Remove from the heat, stir in about two thirds of the grated cheeses, the salt, and a generous grinding of black pepper. Set aside.

2. In a medium skillet over moderate heat, melt the butter. When it foams, stir in the red pepper, jalapeños, garlic, scallions, oregano, and tomatoes. Lower the heat, cover the skillet, and cook, stirring occasionally, for 15 minutes. Uncover the skillet, stir in the crabmeat, and cook for another 5 minutes. Remove from the heat and stir ¾ cup of the cream sauce into the crabmeat mixture.

3. Preheat the oven to 375°F. Dip a tortilla into the cream sauce and lay it in the bottom of a round, individual gratin dish. Spread ¼ cup of the crab mixture over the tortilla. Dip a second tortilla into the sauce and place it over the crabmeat layer. Top with a second ¼ cup of filling and top that filling with a third sauce-dipped tortilla. Repeat with the remaining tortillas, filling, and sauce using three tortillas per dish. Sprinkle the remaining grated cheeses over the stacked enchiladas, dividing evenly. Set the dishes in the oven and bake for about 20 minutes, or until the cheese is browned and bubbling. Garnish with shredded lettuce, chopped scallions and sliced avocado and serve at once.

▼▼▼NOTE: *This is also delicious when 3 cups of shredded cooked chicken is substituted for the crab.*

Mesquite-Grilled Steak and Potato Salad

Serves 4

If this really sounds terrific to you, I suppose you'll fire up the grill just to make the salad. The more practical approach, of course, would be to grill the steak whenever you are grilling something else and plan to have the salad the next day. The Jalapeño Vinegar should steep for at least 48 hours, so plan accordingly.

3 medium boiling potatoes, peeled and sliced
    ¼ inch thick
1 tablespoon salt
¾ cup Jalapeño Vinegar (recipe follows)
1½ pounds medium-rare steak, preferably
    mesquite-grilled
1 cup good-quality olive oil
½ cup sliced scallions (including the green tops)
½ cup finely chopped clean fresh cilantro leaves
Mixed salad greens, such as romaine lettuce,
    watercress, and arugula
2 medium perfectly ripe tomatoes

1. In a medium saucepan, cover the potatoes with cold water. Stir in salt, set the pan over medium heat, and bring to a boil. Cook the potatoes, stirring once or twice, until just tender while still holding their shape, about 4 minutes. Drain immediately.

2. Transfer the hot potatoes to a mixing bowl, sprinkle with 2 tablespoons of the Jalapeño Vinegar, and cool to room temperature.

3. Trim the steak of any fat and cut it across the grain into thin slices. Cut the slices into bite-

size pieces. Add the steak and any juices it has exuded to the bowl with the potatoes. Pour the remaining vinegar and the olive oil over the steak and potatoes and toss gently. Add the scallions and cilantro and toss again. Season with salt to taste.

4. To serve, arrange the salad greens on four plates. Mound the steak salad on the greens, dividing it evenly. Spoon any accumulated dressing from the bowl over each portion. Cut the tomatoes into sixths and garnish each salad with 3 tomato wedges. Serve, passing the pepper mill.

▼▼▼NOTE: *Of course the steak needn't be grilled over mesquite, or anything else for that matter, although the smoky "edge" gives the salad a certain something that raises it out of the ordinary. An excellent accompaniment would be thick-cut garlic bread, the kind that used to be called, for some reason, Texas toast.*

 Jalapeño Vinegar

Makes about 4 cups

4 cups good-quality white wine or champagne
    vinegar
2 medium fresh jalapeños, halved

1. In a medium, noncorrosive saucepan over medium heat, bring the vinegar to a boil.

2. Place the jalapeños in a heatproof storage container. Pour the hot vinegar over the jalapeños, cool to room temperature, cover, and let stand for 48 hours before using.

Chilled White Bean Soup with Lime and Cilantro

Serves 6

Serve this cool but substantial soup in mugs, while you're waiting for the steaks or fajitas to grill.

½ pound Great Northern beans, sorted and
    rinsed
3 tablespoons unsalted butter
1 medium yellow onion, peeled and finely
    chopped
1 large carrot, quartered
1½ teaspoons dried thyme
2 bay leaves
6 cups degreased chicken stock or canned
    chicken broth
1 teaspoon salt
1½ cups buttermilk, approximately
3 to 4 tablespoons fresh lime juice
¾ cup finely chopped clean fresh cilantro leaves

1. In a medium bowl, combine the beans with enough cold water to cover them by at least 2 inches and let soak for 24 hours. Drain.

2. In a 4-quart soup pot, melt the butter over medium heat. Add the onion, carrot, thyme, and bay leaves and cook, covered, stirring once or twice, until the vegetables are tender, about 20 minutes.

3. Add the chicken stock and drained beans to the pot. Raise the heat, bring to a boil, and skim any scum that may form. Lower the heat, partially cover, and simmer, stirring occasionally, for 45 minutes. Stir in the salt and continue to cook until the beans are very tender, another 15 to 20 minutes.

4. Drain the beans, reserving the liquid. Discard the carrot and bay leaves. Puree beans with 1 cup of the cooking liquid in a food processor. Add the remaining liquid and blend until smooth. Transfer the soup to a bowl, stir in 1 cup of the buttermilk, and the lime juice. Cover and refrigerate overnight, or until very cold.

5. To serve, thin as desired with the remaining buttermilk. Taste and correct the seasoning (the soup should be slightly tart) and stir in the cilantro.

Gazpacho

Serves 8

This is a big, gutsy gazpacho, meant to be a meal, not a starter, for lunch or supper on a scorching day. Serve with Calico Corn Muffins (page 95) or garlic bread, or, if it's too hot to turn on the oven, crusty French bread. A simple-minded pink or white wine would be good to drink.

2½ pounds (about 15) ripe Italian plum tomatoes
2 good-size cucumbers
1 large sweet red pepper
1 large sweet green pepper
3 cups chilled tomato juice
1 medium yellow onion, finely diced
⅓ cup good-quality olive oil
3 tablespoons red wine vinegar
2 tablespoons Worcestershire sauce
1 tablespoon Tabasco sauce
1½ tablespoons salt
2 cups Guacamole (page 35)

1. Halve the tomatoes, squeeze out the seeds and juices, and cut the flesh into ½-inch dice.

2. Peel and seed the cucumbers and cut them into ½-inch dice.

3. Stem and core the peppers and cut them into ½-inch dice.

4. In a food processor, combine 1 cup of diced tomato, ½ cup of diced cucumber, and ½ cup diced pepper. Process briefly; then add 2 cups of the tomato juice and process until smooth.

5. Transfer the puree to a bowl and stir in the remaining diced vegetables. Add the onion, oil, vinegar, Worcestershire and Tabasco sauces, and salt. Add additional tomato juice to achieve the desired consistency. Cover and chill the gazpacho overnight.

6. Taste and correct the seasoning. You may want more vinegar, Worcestershire, Tabasco, or salt—the soup should be zesty. Ladle the soup into chilled bowls, and garnish each with a dollop of Guacamole. Serve at once.

Tortilla Soup

Serves 6 to 8

Make this frugal soup from the stock left after poaching a chicken or make it on purpose, using the recipe below. The soup—concocted from a few inexpensive ingredients—is astonishingly flavorful and comforting, the whole, obviously, much greater than the sum of its simple parts.

3 pounds chicken backs and/or wings
12 cups canned chicken broth
2 large yellow onions, peeled and chopped (about
    4 cups)
4 large carrots, peeled and chopped (about
    2 cups)
8 whole garlic cloves, peeled
2 teaspoons dried oregano, preferably Mexican

1 teaspoon dried thyme
12 whole black peppercorns
6 corn tortillas
8 ounces Monterey Jack cheese
Salt
2 medium zucchini, scrubbed and coarsely grated
4 scallions (including the green tops), sliced
¾ cup Salsa Fresca (page 30)

1. In an 8-quart stock pot over medium heat, combine the chicken and chicken broth. Add 4 cups of water and bring to a boil, skimming any scum that forms. Stir in the onions, carrots, garlic, oregano, thyme, and peppercorns. Return to a boil; then cover, lower the heat, and simmer, stirring and skimming occasionally, for 2 hours.

2. Cool slightly and then strain. Discard the solids and refrigerate the broth, covered, overnight.

3. With a sharp knife cut the tortillas into strips about ¼-inch wide. Spread the strips in a shallow pan and leave, uncovered, at room temperature overnight.

4. Cut the Monterey Jack into ¼-inch cubes and let it come to room temperature.

5. Remove the solidified fat from the surface of the broth and discard it. In a soup pot, bring the broth to a simmer. Taste and correct the seasoning. Divide the dried tortilla strips, cheese, zucchini, and scallions among serving bowls. Bring the broth to a full boil. Ladle the hot broth into bowls, spoon a dollop of Salsa Fresca into each bowl, and serve at once.

▼▼▼NOTE: *To make this soup a complete meal, add shredded cooked chicken and cooked rice to each bowl as well. Garnish with diced avocado. If you have no Salsa Fresca, substitute diced ripe tomato and fresh lime juice to taste.*

Posole
Serves 10

Oddly enough for a dish with festival associations
(posole is traditionally served on New Year's Day),
this is about as rough and plain a boiled dinner as
it's possible to find. There may be more subtle
versions of posole than the one below, but I doubt
if they are any more satisfying to eat. As with
much of the authentic southwestern fare, so few
ingredients simmered together seem unlikely to
produce so savory a result—but they do. Unlike
the recipe for Tortilla Soup, the Salsa Fresca is
essential to this dish.

⅓ cup olive oil
4 large yellow onions, peeled and coarsely
    chopped (about 8 cups)
8 medium garlic cloves, peeled and minced
6 to 8 jalapeños, preferably fresh, stemmed and
    minced
1½ tablespoons dried oregano, preferably
    Mexican
3 quarts (12 cups) chicken stock or canned
    chicken broth
4 pounds country-style pork spareribs
3 cans (16 ounces each) hominy, well drained
Salt
3 cups Salsa Fresca (page 30), diced ripe
    avocado, and sliced scallions, as garnish

    1. In a 7- to 8-quart pot over low heat, warm
the oil. Add the onions, garlic, jalapeños, and
oregano. Cover and cook, stirring occasionally, for
20 minutes, or until the vegetables are tender and
lightly colored.
    2. Add the chicken stock and spareribs to
the pot. Raise the heat and bring to a boil, skim-

ming any scum that forms. Partially cover the pan, lower the heat, and simmer, stirring once or twice, for 1 hour.

3. Add the hominy and simmer, partially covered, stirring once or twice, for another hour, or until the meat is falling off the bones.

4. Cool to room temperature, cover, and refrigerate overnight.

5. Lift off and discard the hardened surface fat. Remove the spareribs and bones. Cut any remaining meat off the bones and shred or dice it. Discard the bones. Return the meat to the pot. Set the pot over low heat and bring the broth to a brisk simmer, stirring often. Taste and correct the seasoning.

6. To serve, ladle the posole into wide, deep bowls. Pass the Salsa Fresca, avocado, and scallions and allow guests to garnish each serving as they wish.

▼▼▼NOTE: *Use white or yellow hominy, or a combination. A pig's foot, split and cleaned, will add richness to the posole. Order it from the butcher and discard it when removing the rib meat from the bones. Other possible garnishes include thin-sliced radishes, black olives, and minced clean fresh cilantro leaves.*

Black Bean Soup
Serves 6 to 8

The American Southwest abounds with zesty black bean soups, the best of them combining the rich spices associated with Spanish cooking and the pungent heat of local green chiles. Too thick and hearty to be anything but a main course, this soup is perfectly paired with warm Calico Corn Muffins (page 95) and a cooling green salad. (Make this milder, if you will, but our customers love it just like this.)

¼ cup rendered bacon fat or olive oil
2 large yellow onions, peeled and coarsely
    chopped (about 4 cups)
8 garlic cloves, peeled and minced
3 cups beef stock or canned beef broth
3 cups chicken stock or canned chicken broth
2 cups water
1 pound dried black beans, sorted and rinsed (see
    Note)
1 meaty smoked ham hock or ham bone
1 pig's foot, cleaned and split
3 tablespoons ground cumin, from toasted seeds
2 tablespoons dried oregano, preferably Mexican
1 tablespoon dried thyme
¼ teaspoon ground cloves
4 to 5 vinegar or brine-packed jalapeños en
    escabeche, finely chopped (about ¼ cup), or
    to taste
Salt
Sour cream, diced ripe tomatoes, and sliced
    scallions, as garnish

1. In a 4½- to 5-quart soup pot or Dutch oven, warm the bacon fat over medium heat. Add

the onions and garlic, lower the heat slightly, and cook, covered, stirring once or twice, until tender, about 20 minutes.

2. Add the beef and chicken stocks and water. Stir in the beans, ham hock, pig's foot, cumin, oregano, thyme, cloves, and jalapeños. Raise the heat and bring the soup to a boil; then lower the heat and simmer, partially covered, stirring once or twice and skimming any scum that forms, for about 2 hours, or until the beans are very tender. (If the beans are old they may take longer to cook. Add additional water, ½ cup at a time, and continue to cook, stirring often, until they are tender.)

3. Remove and discard the pig's foot. Remove the ham hock and cool it.

4. In a food processor, puree half the soup. Return the puree to the pot. Remove the skin from the ham hock; then shred the meat and add it to the soup.

5. Taste and correct the seasoning and simmer for another 10 minutes.

6. To serve, ladle the soup into bowls and garnish each serving with a dollop of sour cream and a sprinkling of diced tomato and sliced scallions.

NOTE: *The beans are not soaked. The pig's foot, while not essential, gives the soup a unique richness and shine. Order it from the butcher. The salty nature of several ingredients usually makes additional salt unnecessary.*

Potato-Corn Soup with Chiles and Cheese
Serves 6 to 8

This soup, one of the non-chili items on our very first menu, was later dropped for technical, kitchen reasons, leaving more than a few depressed fans behind. Glitches in a restaurant kitchen ought not to keep home cooks from enjoying this creamy, slightly picante, and utterly satisfying soup, and so here is the recipe. Team it with a green salad and a batch of warm Calico Corn Muffins (page 95) for a first-rate supper.

4 tablespoons unsalted butter
1 large yellow onion, peeled and coarsely
    chopped (about 2 cups)
3 carrots, peeled and chopped (about 1 cup)
4 cups chicken stock or canned chicken broth
1½ pounds potatoes, peeled and cut into 1-inch
    chunks
½ teaspoon cayenne pepper
2 teaspoons salt
1 can (16 ounces) cream-style corn
1 can (27 ounces) whole, fire-roasted mild green
    chiles, drained and cut into ½-inch dice
½ cup milk or half-and-half, approximately
6 ounces medium-sharp Cheddar cheese, grated
6 ounces Monterey Jack cheese, grated

1. In a 4½- to 5-quart soup pot over low heat, melt the butter. Add the onion and carrots and cook, covered, stirring once or twice, for 20 minutes.

2. Add the chicken stock, potatoes, cayenne pepper, and salt and bring to a boil. Lower the heat, cover, and cook, stirring occasionally, for

about 40 minutes, or until the potatoes and carrots are very tender. Cool slightly; then strain the soup, reserving the liquid.

3. Transfer the solids to a food processor and process briefly. Add 1 cup of the reserved liquid to the processor and process until smooth, stopping once to scrape down the sides of the workbowl.

4. Return the puree and the reserved liquid to the soup pot. Set it over low heat and stir in the corn, chiles, and milk. Bring slowly to a simmer. Taste, correct the seasoning, and thin further, if desired, with additional milk. Simmer, stirring often, for 5 minutes.

5. In a medium bowl, toss together the grated cheeses. Ladle the soup into bowls, sprinkle each portion with about ⅓ cup of the cheese, and serve at once.

Savory Spinach and Potato Flan
Serves 9

This dish is for what one critic called ". . . the few pitiful patrons who don't understand chili." In truth, it is somewhat more than just the token mild dish on the menu. A cross between a quiche and the more substantial fritatta-like Mexican or Spanish "omelet," it is rich, tender, and flavorful —in a mild way. Serve it warm or cold for supper or brunch, and if you like things with a little more kick, I suggest Bruce's modification—top each portion with a generous dollop of Salsa Fresca (page 30).

1 pound (8 or 9) new potatoes, scrubbed
1 package (10 ounces) frozen chopped spinach,
    thawed
10 large eggs
1½ teaspoons salt
½ teaspoon ground nutmeg
Pinch of cayenne pepper
4 cups (1 quart) heavy cream
1 cup (about 4 ounces) grated medium-sharp
    Cheddar cheese
1 cup (about 4 ounces) grated Monterey Jack
    cheese

1. Preheat the oven to 350°F. Slice the potatoes very thin, and put them into a medium saucepan, and cover them with cold water. Set over high heat and bring to a boil. Lower the heat and cook for another minute or two, or until the potatoes are just tender while still holding their shape. Drain, rinse gently under cold water, and drain again.

2. Spread half the potatoes in a layer in a 9 × 13-inch baking pan. Squeeze the spinach dry and spread it evenly over the potato layer. Spread the remaining potatoes over the spinach.

3. In a mixing bowl, beat the eggs. Whisk in the salt, nutmeg, and cayenne pepper and then whisk in the cream. Pour the egg mixture gently and evenly over the potatoes and spinach. Sprinkle the grated cheeses evenly over the egg mixture.

4. Bake the flan for 40 to 50 minutes, or until it is evenly puffed and golden brown and the center is firm. Cool almost to room temperature on a wire rack before cutting into squares.

O N THE SIDE

Accompaniments to the basic Bowl of Red are as personal as the concoction of the chili itself. Here are the side dishes we offer at the restaurant —some authentic and some quite personal interpretations of what is needed to turn a bowl of chili into a meal.

◢ Calico Corn Muffins
12 muffins

A bowl of chili is a fairly complete dining experience for many people, and nothing more is required than the presence of some bread for swabbing out the bowl when the last spoonful of chili is gone. In Texas, as often as not, this is a stack of sliced packaged white bread set on a plate in the middle of the table. In our restaurant, it's a basket of tasty, crusty (some say hard as rocks) sourdough rolls. But for a special segment of chili eaters, only a batch of jalapeño-spiced corn bread will do. A moist and steamy batch of these muffins does make a top-notch chili accompaniment, but don't limit them. They add a spicy touch wherever corn bread is appropriate and they make a simple soup or egg dish into a special meal.

1¼ cups stone-ground yellow cornmeal
¾ cup unbleached all-purpose flour
⅓ cup sugar

1 tablespoon baking powder
¼ teaspoon baking soda
¼ teaspoon salt
1 large egg
⅔ cup buttermilk at room temperature
⅓ cup finely diced pimiento
2 jalapeños en escabeche, stemmed and minced
1 cup frozen corn kernels, thawed
6 tablespoons unsalted butter, melted

1. Preheat the oven to 400°F. Lightly butter a 12-cup muffin tin.

2. In a large mixing bowl, combine well the cornmeal, flour, sugar, baking powder, baking soda, and salt. In a small bowl, beat the egg thoroughly, then whisk in the buttermilk.

3. In a strainer under cold water, rinse the pimiento and jalapeños thoroughly. Add the corn to the strainer and press hard with the back of a spoon to extract as much moisture as possible.

4. Add the buttermilk mixture, the pimiento mixture, and the melted butter to the bowl with the dry ingredients and stir until just combined.

5. Spoon the batter into the prepared pan, dividing it evenly and filling the cups about three-quarters full. Set on an oven rack in the middle of the oven and bake for about 25 minutes, or until the muffins are golden brown.

6. Turn the muffins out of the tin at once and serve them with butter while they are still warm.

▼▼▼ NOTE: *You can also spoon the batter into a buttered 9 × 9-inch baking pan and extend the cooking time by about 10 minutes. Cut into squares and serve warm. Day-old muffins can be split and toasted, and they reheat in a microwave oven beautifully.*

Lime Salad Dressing
Makes about 2½ cups

A smooth and creamy, but tart, dressing, useful on any number of salads. Our house green salad is a combination of tender inner romaine lettuce leaves and watercress, garnished with shredded jícama, orange sections, rings of red onion, and diced ripe tomatoes.

3 large eggs
¼ cup fresh lime juice, approximately
1 tablespoon mild whole-grain mustard,
     preferably imported
Minced zest of 2 limes
1 teaspoon salt
Freshly ground black pepper
1 cup olive oil
1 cup corn or other flavorless oil

    1. In a food processor fitted with a steel blade, combine the eggs, lime juice, mustard, lime zest, and salt. Season generously with pepper and process for 1 minute.
    2. With the motor running, add the olive and corn oils in a quick, steady stream. When all the oil has been added, shut the motor off at once.
    3. Taste and correct the seasoning, adding more lime juice if the dressing lacks tartness. Re-process to blend, transfer to a storage container, cover, and refrigerate. Allow the dressing to return to room temperature before using.

Creamy Coleslaw
Serves 6

Beginning restaurateurs are advised to "pay attention to details," an axiom we took to heart. Still, we never expected to become famous for our coleslaw! Its popularity stems, I think, from its balance of sweet and tart, and from its coarse, hearty texture. It is, as we say on our menu, crunchy and cooling, and there are, indeed, those who can't imagine a bowl of chili without a bowl of coleslaw nearby.

1 cup mayonnaise
1 cup sour cream
½ cup mild whole-grain mustard, preferably imported
¼ cup strained fresh lemon juice
3 tablespoons sugar
1 white cabbage (about 2 pounds)
3 large carrots
2 crisp, tart apples

1. In a medium bowl, whisk together the mayonnaise, sour cream, mustard, lemon juice, and sugar.

2. Remove any wilted outer leaves of cabbage; then core and quarter the cabbage. With a long, sharp knife cut the quarters into ⅛-inch julienne. You should have about 6 cups.

3. Peel the carrots and cut them into lengths that just fit crosswise in the feed tube of a food processor. With the coarsest shredding blade in place, grate the carrots. Wash and core the apples and cut them into quarters. Grate the apples, fitting them crosswise in the feed tube.

4. In a large bowl, combine the shredded cabbage, carrots, and apples. Add all the dressing

and toss thoroughly. Cover and refrigerate overnight to let the slaw marinate. When serving, pass
the pepper mill.

▼▼▼NOTE: *A good, unsweetened commercial mayonnaise is acceptable in this recipe, although if
you use homemade you will get a superior slaw.
We use Temeraire French mustard, since it comes
in big, convenient cans, but the Pommery brand is
more widely available. Don't be tempted to shred
the cabbage with the processor or to use a hand
grater on the apples and carrots—the texture of
the slaw will be wrong.*

 # Drunken Beans
Serves 6 to 8

This side dish was meant to provide the beans for
those who like them anywhere but in the chili. Try
them as an accompaniment to a batch of, say, The
Real McCoy (page 44). Serve them alongside a
grilled steak and a salad of sliced tomatoes, or
team them with scrambled eggs, salsa, and corn
bread for a hearty breakfast. (You may also, as I
do, find them good enough to eat all alone, with
just a few flour tortillas for scooping—as simple
and comforting a dish as it's possible to imagine.)

3 cups beef stock or canned beef broth
3 cups chicken stock or canned chicken broth
1 bottle (12 ounces) dark beer
1 pound dried pinto beans, sorted and rinsed (see
     Note)
1 medium onion, peeled and coarsely chopped
     (about 2 cups)
6 medium garlic cloves, peeled and minced
½ pound slab bacon

99

3 jalapeños, preferably fresh, stemmed and
minced
1½ tablespoons dried oregano, preferably
Mexican
1 can (28 ounces) Italian plum tomatoes, crushed
and well drained
1 teaspoon salt
Sour cream and sliced scallions, as garnish

1. In a 4½- to 5-quart flameproof casserole
or Dutch oven, combine the beef and chicken
stocks, dark beer, pinto beans, onion, and garlic.
Set the pan over medium heat. Remove the rind
from the bacon, add the rind to the pan with the
beans, and bring to a boil. Skim any scum that
forms, lower the heat, cover, and cook, stirring
occasionally, for 1 hour.

2. Meanwhile, cut the remaining bacon into
¼-inch cubes. Set a skillet over medium heat, add
the bacon, and cook, stirring once or twice, until
the bacon is brown and crisp, about 20 minutes.
Lower the heat, stir in the jalapeños and oregano,
and cook for 5 minutes. Mix in the tomatoes and
cook, stirring, for another 5 minutes. Remove
from the heat and reserve.

3. After the beans have cooked for 1 hour,
stir in the bacon mixture and salt. Continue to
simmer the beans, uncovered, stirring often, for
another hour, or until they are just tender. Discard
the bacon rind. Serve the beans topped with a
dollop of sour cream and a sprinkling of sliced
scallions.

▼▼▼NOTE: *The beans are not soaked. For best results select a dark beer that is slightly sweet (as
opposed to bitter), such as Beck's, Heineken, or the
excellent American beer Double Dark Prior's.
Mexican dark beers are a bit too light for cooking
with the beans.*

SWEETS

If you doubt that chili is a truly American dish, ask yourself what you want for dessert afterward. While there is a wonderful repertoire of authentic southwestern desserts, most people turn to sturdy, homemade American-style sweets when the chili's gone. Nothing else quite concludes a chili meal appropriately, and we have never regretted our decision to leave the authentic desserts to others.

Chocolate-Peanut Butter Mousse

Serves 8

Culinary jingoism aside, the best milk chocolate is Belgian. While it's hardly a requirement for this dessert, as with most cookery, the better ingredient yields the better result. This mousse was a bit of a sleeper when we first added it to the menu, but its candy bar flavors soon won it a steady following.

10 ounces best-quality milk chocolate, chopped
½ cup unsalted chunky peanut butter
1 cup heavy cream
3 large eggs at room temperature
¼ cup sugar
1 cup heavy cream, whipped to soft peaks, and
⅓ cup whole hulled peanuts, as garnish

1. Construct a modified double boiler by setting a good-size heavy ceramic mixing bowl (I use my bread bowl) over a saucepan of water. The bottom of the bowl should just touch the water.

2. Combine the chopped chocolate and peanut butter in the bowl, set the "double boiler" over low heat and leave it there, stirring occasionally, until the chocolate has just melted, about 10 minutes. Do not let the water boil.

3. Meanwhile, whip the cream in a small bowl to the point just *before* it will hold a soft peak. Set aside.

4. Separate the eggs, putting the yolks in a small bowl and the whites in a medium bowl. With a fork, whisk the sugar slowly into the egg yolks. Set aside. With a whisk, beat the whites to the point just *before* they will hold a soft peak. Set aside.

5. Remove the bowl with the melted chocolate from the pan of hot water and transfer it to a work surface. Add the egg yolk mixture all at once and whisk vigorously. With a large rubber spatula, scrape the beaten cream into the chocolate. Stir well, without fear of deflating, until the chocolate and cream are well combined. Scrape the beaten whites on top of this mixture and gently fold together until just combined. (A few random streaks of white are not a problem.)

6. Transfer the mousse to a large bowl or divide among individual serving dishes, such as custard cups or pots de crème. Refrigerate until the tops are set, about 30 minutes; then cover and chill until firm, about 2 hours for individual portions or 5 hours for a large bowl.

7. To serve, garnish with whipped cream and a sprinkle of peanuts.

◉ Triple Citrus Ice

About 1½ quarts, serving 6 to 8

Tart, cool, and utterly soothing to the chili-ravaged palate.

2 cups sugar
2 cups water
Finely minced zest of 1 lime, 1 lemon, and 1
    navel orange
2 cups strained fresh citrus juice (approximately
    equal parts lime, lemon, and orange juice)

    1. In a small, heavy saucepan, combine the sugar, water, and minced zest. Set the pan over medium heat and bring the mixture to a boil, stirring often to dissolve the sugar. Pour the syrup into a heatproof bowl and cool to room temperature. Stir in the citrus juices and refrigerate, covered, until very cold, at least 5 hours and preferably overnight.

    2. Churn the chilled mixture in an ice-cream maker according to the manufacturer's directions. Transfer the ice to a storage container, cover, and freeze until ready to serve. Let the ice soften in the refrigerator for 10 to 15 minutes, if necessary, before serving.

▼▼▼ NOTE: *Different types of ice-cream makers will produce different quantities of ice. For a particularly brisk and palate-clearing effect, drizzle each serving of the ice with a tablespoon of gold tequila just before serving.*

Mississippi Mud

Serves 9 to 100

When Craig Claiborne mentioned Mississippi Mud in the *New York Times,* he received a flood of nostalgic mail and recipes from Southerners affectionately homesick for this classic sweet. From the many recipes he distilled the quintessential Mississippi Mud, and it is his version that we have adapted for the restaurant. Our menu calls it dangerously chocolate. It might also be called dangerously sweet, even though most of my modifications have been in the sugar department. We cut a pan of this into nine pieces, but people always share. You might consider doing what I did for one catered event and cut the Mud into 1-inch squares. Tell guests it's candy!

Cake

1 cup unbleached all-purpose flour
¾ cup *packed* cocoa, *not* Dutch process
½ teaspoon salt
½ pound unsalted butter, softened
1½ cups granulated sugar
4 large eggs
1 teaspoon vanilla extract
3 ounces (about 1 cup) pecans, coarsely chopped
3 cups miniature marshmallows

Icing

½ cup *packed* cocoa, *not* Dutch process
2¼ cups confectioners' sugar
½ pound unsalted butter, softened
3 to 4 tablespoons buttermilk
3 ounces (about 1 cup) pecans, coarsely chopped

1. Preheat the oven to 350°F. Butter and flour a 9 × 13-inch baking pan and tap out the excess flour.

2. To make the cake, sift together the flour, cocoa, and salt.

3. In a medium bowl, cream the butter and granulated sugar until light and fluffy. Beat in the eggs, one at a time, beating well after each addition. Stir in the vanilla. Fold in the sifted mixture until it is nearly incorporated. The batter will be thick. Add the pecans and stir until they are just combined.

4. Spoon the batter into the prepared pan and spread evenly to the sides of the pan. Bake for 15 minutes. (The edges of the cake will appear done, but the center will be quite raw.)

5. Slide the oven rack out slightly. Working quickly, sprinkle the marshmallows evenly over the cake. Return the cake to the oven and bake for another 5 minutes, or until the marshmallows are just melted and becoming golden brown. Set the cake on a wire rack and cool completely.

6. For the icing, sift together the cocoa and confectioners' sugar. In a medium bowl, cream the butter. Stir the sifted mixture 1 cup at a time into the butter, moistening as needed with tablespoons of buttermilk. Spread the icing evenly over the cooled cake, using all of it. Sprinkle the chopped pecans evenly over the icing.

7. Refrigerate the cake, covered, until ready to serve. Let stand at room temperature for about 10 minutes before cutting. Let the cake come completely to room temperature before serving.

▼▼▼NOTE: *If you have ever doubted sugar is a preservative, this cake will change your mind. Well wrapped and refrigerated, it keeps at least a week.*

Apple-Rum-Raisin Crisp

Serves 8 to 10

The fruit crisp changes on a weekly basis, taking advantage of whatever is freshest and most interesting in the market. Over the seasons, apple crisps have been made more than any others, and among them this very adult combination remains the most popular.

Crust

1 cup unbleached all-purpose flour
1 cup (3 ounces) pecans
¾ cup packed light brown sugar
12 tablespoons unsalted butter, chilled

Filling

¾ cup golden raisins
½ cup dark rum
3 pounds (6 or 7) Granny Smith apples
½ cup granulated sugar
⅓ cup unbleached all-purpose flour
1 tablespoon vanilla extract
Sour cream, vanilla ice cream, or whipped
    cream, as optional accompaniment

    1. To make the crust, combine the flour with the pecans and sugar in a food processor and process with brief pulses until well combined. Cut the butter into small pieces, add it to the processor, and process for about 45 seconds, or until a lumpy dough is formed. Transfer the dough to a bowl, cover, and refrigerate.
    2. To make the filling, combine the raisins and rum in a small heavy saucepan. Set over low heat and bring just to a boil. Remove from the heat and let stand, stirring once or twice, until cool.

3. Core and peel the apples and cut them into ½-inch pieces. In a large bowl, toss the apples with the sugar and flour. Stir in the raisins, any unabsorbed rum, and the vanilla and toss again. Let the apples stand at room temperature 30 minutes. Preheat the oven to 400°F.

4. Spoon the apple mixture and any juices into a shallow baking dish just large enough to hold it—a 9 × 14-inch oval gratin dish or a 9 × 13-inch rectangular baking dish will do. With a fork, coarsely crumble the chilled topping. Sprinkle it evenly over the apples (it will look like a lot of topping, but use it all anyway).

5. Set the dish on an oven rack in the lower third of the oven and bake for 35 to 45 minutes, or until the topping is well browned and the filling is bubbling gently.

6. Cool on a wire rack. Serve warm or at room temperature, with sour cream (first choice), ice cream, whipped cream, or as is.

▼▼▼ NOTE: *Omit the rum if you wish. You may then use the raisins or not, just stirring them into the apples along with the sugar and flour, and seasoning the filling with 1½ teaspoons of ground cinnamon and ½ teaspoon of ground nutmeg.*

Butterscotch Bread Pudding
Serves 9

Words fail.

2 large, fresh loaves whole wheat bread (see
    Note)
4 large eggs
½ cup plus 1 tablespoon sugar
4½ cups heavy cream
1½ tablespoons vanilla extract
Butterscotch Sauce (recipe follows)

1. Preheat the oven to 325°F. With a serrated knife remove any tough crusts from the bread and cut the bread into 1-inch cubes. You should have 10 cups of cubes.

2. In a mixing bowl, whisk the eggs thoroughly. Gradually whisk in the ½ cup sugar; then whisk in the cream and vanilla. Add the bread cubes and stir once or twice, to just coat the bread with the egg mixture. Spoon immediately into a 9 × 13-inch baking pan, spreading the cubes of bread evenly to the edges of the pan. Pour the remaining egg mixture over the cubes and sprinkle the remaining tablespoon of sugar evenly over the top of the pudding.

3. Bake for 40 to 50 minutes, or until evenly puffed and the edges of the bread cubes are a rich brown. The center of the pudding should be just set.

4. Cool on a wire rack almost to room temperature before attempting to cut. The pudding will be fragile. Transfer pieces to dessert plates, spoon warmed Butterscotch Sauce over each, and serve at once.

▼▼▼NOTE: *Something sturdier than supermarket bread is required here for the proper effect. We buy the excellent Italian whole wheat from Zito's bakery, just down the street. Those not able to shop on Bleecker Street should look for a good ethnic bakery or health food store that stocks unsliced breads. If you find good-quality white bread, instead of whole wheat, by all means use it.*

Butterscotch Sauce
Makes about 2 cups

Better than anything you can buy (cheaper, too) and too good to limit to bread pudding. Try the sauce on waffles, baked apples, coffee ice cream . . .

8 tablespoons unsalted butter
1 cup packed light brown sugar
⅓ cup corn syrup
1½ cups heavy cream
1 tablespoon vanilla extract
1 teaspoon strained fresh lemon juice

1. In a heavy medium saucepan over moderate heat, melt the butter and sugar together. Stir in the corn syrup. Whisk in the heavy cream, raise the heat, and bring just to a boil. Lower the heat slightly and simmer briskly, stirring occasionally with a metal spoon to reduce the risk of boiling over, for 15 minutes, or until thickened slightly.
2. Remove from the heat, stir in the vanilla and lemon juice, and transfer immediately to a heatproof storage container. Cool to room temperature, cover, and refrigerate. The sauce will keep well, refrigerated, for several weeks.
3. To use, stir to recombine if the sauce has separated; then warm gently over low heat, stirring often.

Coconut-Lime Cheesecake
Serves 10 to 12

There are as many cheesecake recipes as there are stars in the heavens, or something like that. Of all the versions I have tried out on the menu over the last two years this remains the most popular. It is moist and creamy (as opposed to dry and sticky), and is topped with sour cream in what I think of as the midwestern style. Someone once told me New Yorkers wouldn't eat this kind of cheesecake. He was wrong.

Crust

1 cup graham cracker crumbs
¼ cup sugar
4 tablespoons unsalted butter, melted

Filling

1½ pounds cream cheese at room temperature
1½ cups sugar
¼ cup fresh lime juice
Finely minced zest of 2 limes
4 large eggs

Topping

1 pint sour cream
⅓ cup sugar
2 tablespoons fresh lime juice
Finely minced zest of 2 limes
1½ cups sweetened flaked coconut, toasted (see
　　Note)

　　1. Preheat the oven to 350°F. For the crust, in a small bowl toss together the crumbs, sugar, and melted butter until evenly combined. Pat

firmly into a 10-inch springform pan and refrigerate.

2. For the filling, combine all the ingredients in a food processor fitted with a metal blade and process until smooth, stopping once to scrape down the sides of the workbowl.

3. Pour the filling into the prepared pan, set on an oven rack in the middle of the oven, and bake about 40 minutes, or until the edges are just lightly browned and pulling away from the side of the pan. The center of the cake will still be slightly unset.

4. While the cake bakes, prepare the topping. In a small bowl, whisk together the sour cream, sugar, lime juice, and zest.

5. Slide the rack partway out of the oven, leaving the cheesecake on the rack. Working quickly, spoon the topping over the cake, beginning with the edges. (The topping should fill the slight gap between the pan and the edge of the cake.) Smooth the topping and sprinkle the toasted coconut evenly over it.

6. Return the rack to the oven and bake the cheesecake for another 10 minutes, or until the edges of the topping are bubbling slightly.

7. Cool the cake to room temperature on a wire rack. Cover and refrigerate overnight, or until very cold. Cut the cheesecake with a long, thin knife dipped in cold water, wiping the knife after each cut.

▼▼▼NOTE: *To toast coconut, preheat the oven to 400°F. Spread the coconut in a shallow pan (like a pie pan) and bake about 10 minutes, stirring once or twice, or until golden brown. The cheesecake is equally good made with orange juice and minced orange zest. Use the coconut topping or not, as you wish.*

Margarita Pie
Serves 8

This tangy, fresh lime pie comes up from the Keys —by way of Mexico. Serve it with lots of unsweetened whipped cream.

Crust

1¼ cups graham cracker crumbs
¼ cup sugar
4 tablespoons unsalted butter, melted

Filling

7 large eggs
8 large egg yolks
1½ cups sugar
1⅓ cups fresh lime juice (about 9 limes)
Finely grated zest of 1 lime
8 tablespoons unsalted butter, cut into small
    pieces
½ cup tequila, preferably Cuervo Gold
⅓ cup Cointreau
1 cup heavy cream, whipped to soft peaks, as
    garnish

    1. For the crust, in a small bowl toss together the crumbs, sugar, and melted butter until evenly combined. Pat evenly and firmly into a 10-inch pie pan and refrigerate.

    2. For the filling, in a small heavy-bottomed, noncorrosive saucepan, whisk together the eggs and egg yolks. Gradually whisk in the sugar, lime juice, and zest.

    3. Set over low heat and cook, stirring constantly, until the mixture thickens enough to heavily coat the back of a spoon. This happens rather suddenly, after about 9 minutes of cooking.

4. Remove from the heat immediately and stir in the butter all at once. Whisk until the butter is incorporated. Stir in the tequila and Cointreau and pour immediately into the prepared crust.

5. Chill until set before covering loosely. Refrigerate overnight before cutting.

▼▼▼ NOTE: *This was a pudding before I turned it into a pie, and while making a graham cracker crust can hardly be called troublesome, you can simplify your life even further by simply spooning the lime mixture, immediately after stirring in the two liquors, into individual pudding or custard cups. Chilling time will then be cut to 2 hours. Whipped cream remains the appropriate garnish.*

Kahlúa Crème Brûlée
Serves 8

From the day we opened this has been our most popular dessert. There is almost no menu (except, perhaps, a very eggy one), either simple or elaborate, that this tender coffee custard with its crackly brown sugar crust doesn't conclude with style.

7 large egg yolks
¼ cup sugar
4 cups heavy cream
1 tablespoon freeze-dried instant coffee granules
½ cup Kahlúa liqueur
1 tablespoon vanilla extract
⅔ cup packed light brown sugar

1. Position an oven rack in the center of the oven and preheat the oven to 325°F. In a medium bowl, whisk together the egg yolks and sugar.

2. In a medium saucepan, stir together the heavy cream and coffee. Set over medium heat and bring to a boil, stirring to dissolve the coffee granules.

3. Slowly whisk the hot cream into the yolks. Whisk in the Kahlúa and vanilla. Ladle the mixture into 8 round shallow broiler-proof serving dishes about 3 inches wide and about 1 inch deep. Set the dishes in a shallow baking pan. Add boiling water to the pan to come halfway up the sides of the dishes.

4. Bake until the tops are set, about 30 minutes. The custards will remain jiggly until they are completely chilled. Remove from the water bath and cool to room temperature. Cover and chill overnight.

5. Preheat the broiler. With your fingers, press the brown sugar through a strainer onto the custards in an even, fluffy layer. Wipe any excess sugar from the edges of the dishes.

6. Broil 5 to 6 inches from the heat source until the sugar liquefies and begins to caramelize, rotating dishes to brown evenly and watching carefully to avoid burning. Refrigerate the finished crème brûlée at least 1 hour before serving.

▼▼▼NOTE: *The custards, without their brown sugar topping, can be refrigerated for up to 3 days before broiling. Once topped, they should be served within 6 hours or so, or before they begin to liquefy. (They're still good this way, as our waiters who get to eat them have learned; they're just not as dramatic.)*

MAIL-ORDER SOURCES

A few thorough mail-order sources are all one needs for the less-common ingredients called for in this book. Send for a current catalog or price list before ordering.

Santa Cruz Chili & Spice Company
Box 177
Tumacacori, AZ 65640
(Mild and hot unseasoned chili powders, chili paste, bottled salsas, and sauces.)

Casados Farms
Box 1269
San Juan Pueblo, NM 87566
(Unseasoned chili powder, blue corn, Mexican oregano, corn husks, pine nuts, and chile ristras.)

Casa Moneo
210 West 14 Street
New York, NY 10011
(Virtually everything necessary for any Mexican, Tex- Mex, or Latin American cooking.)

Aphrodesia
282 Bleecker Street
New York, NY 10014
(High-quality herbs and spices, including chili powders, cayenne, and whole cumin seeds.)

Horticultural Enterprises
Box 34082
Dallas, TX 75231
(Seeds for virtually every kind of pepper, mild or hot, that the home gardener might want.)

Wilderness Gourmet
Box 3257-C
Ann Arbor, MI 48106
(Venison, buffalo, and other game by mail.)

CHILI SOCIETIES

Joiners will appreciate the variety of philosophies espoused by the three major chili groups. Membership dues are modest and usually include subscriptions to the organizations' newsletters. Write for full information.

Chili Appreciation Society International
Box 31183
Dallas, TX 75231

International Chili Society
Box 2966
Newport Beach, CA 92663

International Connoisseurs of Green and Red Chile
Box 3467
Las Cruces, NM 88003

CHILI PERIODICALS

Chili lovers will not want to be without the following important publications. Write for full information.

Goat Gap Gazette
5110 Bayard Lane #2
Houston, TX 77006

Garlic Times
526 Santa Barbara
Berkeley, CA 94707

ACKNOWLEDGMENTS

A restaurant is a collective enterprise and thanking everyone who supported us in our crazy venture from the beginning would be impossible. The list is a long one indeed, and doing justice to them all would take a document the size of a medium city's telephone book.

That said, there are a few names without which any discussion of The Manhattan Chili Co. would be incomplete. They know, as well as we, why they are here, and we thank them for it: J. C. and Carol Brotherhood and Co.; Tom and Kathi Bramlett; Gail Henklein; Francine Maroukian; Darrell Beasley; Abu Ahmed; Fred Strauss, Dennis Jansson and Jim Phillips; Warren Fabrizio; Matthew Pincus; Zack Hanle; everyone at *The COOK'S Magazine*; Bob Shell; Hartley Bernstein; Bob Mazurkiewicz; Bob Bacheler; Andrew Jennetti; and Ken Freeman.

Thanks to Susan Lescher and Pam Thomas, who labored long and hard on the various nuts and bolts of this book.

Special thanks to our staff of waiters, bartenders, busboys, cooks, dishwashers, and delivery boys, who do the work and rarely share the credit.

Very special thanks to Nancy DePaulo and Duncan Osborne, who, in addition to serving as guard dogs, camp counselors, and private confessors, help refine and produce this food in the real world and on a daily basis.

Many thanks indeed to John Duffy, without whose enthusiasm, sense of humor, and talented hammer, the joint would never have been built.

And finally, very special unlimited thanks to our parents—Sally, Fred, Jerry, Shifra, Jim, and Shirley —angels of all sorts, for their love and support.

117

INDEX